30 MINUTE
COOKBOOK

30 MINUTE
COOKBOOK

over 220 dishes you can cook in
less than half an hour

JENNI FLEETWOOD

HERMES
HOUSE

This edition is published by Hermes House

Hermes House is an imprint of Anness Publishing Ltd
Hermes House, 88–89 Blackfriars Road, London SE1 8HA
tel. 020 7401 2077; fax 020 7633 9499; info@anness.com

© Anness Publishing Ltd 1998, 2005

A CIP catalogue record for this book is available from the British Library.

Publisher: Joanna Lorenz
Senior Editor: Linda Fraser
Designer: Ian Sandom
Jacket Design: Lisa Tai
Indexer: Hilary Bird
Photography: Karl Adamson, Steve Baxter, William Lingwood, Patrick McLeavey and Tom Odulate
Recipes: Alex Barker, Kit Chan, Christine France, Sarah Gates, Shirley Gill, Soheila Kimberley,
Elisabeth Lambert Ortiz, Maggie Pannell and Hilaire Walden

Previously published as *The Ultimate 30 Minute Cookbook*

1 3 5 7 9 10 8 6 4 2

NOTES

Standard spoon and cup measures are level.

Large eggs are used unless otherwise stated.

CONTENTS

Introduction *6*

Quick-cooking Techniques *8*

Mix and Match Menus *10*

10 MINUTE RECIPES *12*

10 Minute Soups, Starters and Snacks *14*

10 Minute Poultry and Meat Dishes *32*

10 Minute Fish and Seafood Dishes *43*

10 Minute Pasta *50*

10 Minute Salads and Vegetable Dishes *56*

10 Minute Desserts *78*

20 MINUTE RECIPES *92*

20 Minute Soups, Starters and Snacks *94*

20 Minute Poultry and Meat Dishes *112*

20 Minute Fish and Seafood Dishes *126*

20 Minute Vegetarian Dishes *146*

20 Minute Pasta and Rice Dishes *158*

20 Minute Desserts *164*

30 MINUTE RECIPES *172*

30 Minute Soups, Starters and Snacks *174*

30 Minute Poultry and Meat Dishes *188*

30 Minute Fish and Seafood Dishes *205*

30 Minute Vegetarian Dishes *224*

30 Minute Desserts *238*

Index *252*

INTRODUCTION

Today's hectic lifestyle means that most people have less and less time to spend in the kitchen. After a hard day, either at work or at home, few of us feel inclined to spend hours slaving over a hot stove – or even a hot microwave. Paradoxically, however, we do all want interesting, well presented, healthy meals that are colourful and full of flavour.

So what's the solution? Do you pop into your nearest supermarket and stock up on those expensive ready-prepared meals or do you build up a repertoire of fast, easy dishes that can be made in the brief moments between getting in from work or returning from the school run and whizzing out again?

That's where we come in. For this book, we've assembled as fine a collection of quick cook

recipes as you could find anywhere. For the ultimate fast food, turn to those in the first section that take less than ten minutes. Even the longest recipe in the book can be completed in half an hour – and you can't say fairer than that.

Of course, precisely how long each dish will actually take depends on a number of factors: the competence of the cook; the distractions (children, pets, partners); and how many glasses of wine are consumed in the process. Some dishes benefit from being chilled or marinated if time permits, but when time is short, simply skip these options.

Preparation and cooking times for each recipe are given as a guide. Where these are inextricably linked, as when the cook puts on a pan of pasta, then use the time while it cooks to

prepare the vegetables for a sauce, a single time is given.

Master a few favourite recipes and you're ready for the next challenge – the thirty minute menu! Some suggestions for mix-and-match dishes are given in the pages that follow, together with techniques for basic recipes that are infinitely adaptable.

QUICK COOK SHORT CUTS
The canny cook cheats. Digging your own potatoes or picking and podding your own peas are both admirable pursuits, and the results are doubtless delicious, but for fabulous fast food what you really need is a first class supermarket, which will do the hard work for you. It is now possible to buy a huge range of vegetables and fruits that are ready to cook, from trimmed fine beans and mangetouts to carrot batons and sliced leeks.

Most types of fruit are easy enough to prepare, but look out for ready-sliced, fresh pineapple, mango and melon – fresh and tasty, without the fuss.

Salad leaves are available in astonishing variety – not cheap, but wonderfully convenient for the quick cook – and there's an equally wide range of ready-made dressings, if you can't spare a few minutes to make one of your own.

If it's medleys you're after, you'll find them too. Packets of prepared mixed vegetables are widely available, and where once you would be lucky to find

Left: Quick-cook savoury staples include flour, dried pulses, bottled and canned capers, tomatoes and vegetables, fresh fruit and vegetables, wine, oils and vinegars, garlic, fresh herbs, and eggs.

a single stir-fry mix there are now Thai, Chinese and other Oriental mixtures. The stir-fry vegetables may even come with a sauce, so for a quick main course, all you need to do is stock up with strips of chicken breast, pork fillet or rump steak.

Of course, if cooking is reduced to putting together assorted packages, it isn't very satisfying. The trick is to add extra ingredients of your own to give the dish a unique signature. Herbs, spices, sauces and flavourings like fresh root ginger can make the difference between a dish that tastes like it came off an assembly line and one that has everyone begging for the recipe.

If meat is to be cooked very quickly, it must be very tender. Turkey escalopes are ideal, especially if they are beaten out thinly, then crumbed or simply cooked in a tasty sauce. Liver (calf's or lamb's) is equally appropriate, and has the added advantage of being a good source of iron.

Fish is the original fast food: skinned fillets need no preparation and cook extremely quickly, as does shellfish. The well-stocked store cupboard should include cans of tuna, anchovies and salmon – all staples that can be used to create quick meals.

So – next stop, the grocery section. Even here, there has been a revolution. Once upon a time, canned tomatoes meant whole fruits in a thin, pippy

Right: Store cupboard essentials for desserts include sugar, cocoa powder, home-made chocolate sauce, meringues, fresh fruit, biscuits, nuts, bottled and canned fruits, and eggs.

liquid. Today, the tomatoes are usually chopped, and you can get them with herbs, garlic, chopped peppers and chillies. Passata and puréed tomatoes, which are sold in jars or cans, and tubes of tomato paste or garlic paste, are equally useful.

Also invaluable are cans or jars of fruit, pimientos, chillies, artichoke hearts, beans and other pulses, pesto and olive tapenade. Of course, some of these ingredients cost a little more, but convenience never came without a price.

From the chiller cabinet, you'll need fresh eggs, cream, yogurt, cheeses, butter and margarine, and pastry.

What else? Obviously, you'll need all the staples like flour, sugar, raising agents and rice. Trifle sponges, boudoir biscuits and slabs of gingerbread are first

steps to simple sweets, and ready-to-top pizza bases and tortillas save time and effort.

When it comes to pasta, buy the fresh product if possible, as it not only tastes superb but also cooks in just a few minutes. Dried pasta that cooks in under ten minutes is also widely available, in shapes and strands.

This book is very much in line with modern trends in cooking. We've had the ready-meal revolution, and while these dishes remain a mainstay for many busy families, there has been a swing back to "real" food. We may have neither the time nor the inclination to spend hours on complicated cooking procedures, but we still want to watch food cooking, relish the aromas, hear the meat sizzle in the pan. This collection of recipes promises all that – and in next to no time.

QUICK-COOKING TECHNIQUES

Every quick cook needs a few basics that can be mixed and matched to make a meal in moments. In the savoury stakes, the prime candidate has to be home-made tomato sauce. Use it to top pasta or a scone pizza; mix it with sliced smoked sausages; or spoon it over grilled steaks or chicken breasts. Alternatively, spice it up with chillies and serve topped with a fried egg or pour it over cauliflower or beans, sprinkle with grated cheese and grill until golden.

QUICK SCONE PIZZA

Preparation time 10 minutes
Cooking time 20 minutes

SERVES 4–6
115g/4oz/1 cup self-raising
white flour
115g/4oz/1 cup self-raising
wholemeal flour
pinch of salt
50g/2oz/¼ cup butter, diced
about 150ml/¼ pint/⅔ cup milk
1 quantity of tomato sauce (see
recipe right)
toppings of own choice

1 Preheat the oven to 220°C/ 425°F/Gas 7. Mix the flours and salt in a bowl. Rub in the butter. Add the milk and mix to a dough.

2 Knead the dough gently until smooth, then roll it out and line a 30 x 18cm/12 x 7in Swiss roll tin, pushing up the edges to form a rim. Spread with the tomato sauce and add your favourite toppings. Bake for about 20 minutes.

TOMATO SAUCE

Preparation time 10 minutes
Cooking time 20 minutes

MAKES ABOUT 300ML/½ PINT/1¼ CUPS
15ml/1 tbsp olive oil
1 onion, finely chopped
1 garlic clove, crushed
400g/14oz can chopped tomatoes
15ml/1 tbsp tomato purée
15ml/1 tbsp chopped fresh
mixed herbs
pinch of sugar
salt and ground black pepper

1 Heat the oil in a pan, add the onion and garlic and fry over a gentle heat for 5 minutes, stirring occasionally, until softened.

2 Add the tomatoes, then stir in the tomato purée, fresh mixed herbs, sugar and salt and ground black pepper to taste.

3 Bring to the boil, then simmer, uncovered, over a medium heat for about 15 minutes, stirring occasionally, until the mixture has reduced to a thick pulp. Leave to cool, then cover the sauce and chill until ready to use.

COOKING PASTA

Preparation time nil
Cooking time 3–12 minutes

SERVES 4
350g/12oz pasta
salt
30ml/2 tbsp olive oil or a knob of
butter, to serve

1 Bring a large saucepan of lightly salted water to the boil. Add the pasta and stir to separate the strands or shapes.

2 Cook at a rolling boil until the pasta is tender but still firm to the bite. When halved, shapes must be cooked through.

3 Drain the pasta well in a colander, shaking it hard to remove the excess water. Tip into a bowl and add a drizzle of olive oil or a knob of butter and then scatter over a little grated Parmesan or add your favourite sauce.

COOK'S TIP
Always cook pasta in plenty of water in a large pan to prevent it sticking.

Three more great basics: pancakes can be served simply, with lemon and caster sugar, but are even tastier with home-made chocolate sauce or raspberry purée, either of which can also be used to top ice cream, meringues or fruit. Raspberry purée is also delicious spooned over slices of brioche that have been soaked in egg and cream, then fried in butter.

PERFECT PANCAKES

Preparation time 5 minutes
Cooking time 20 minutes

MAKES ABOUT 12
175g/6oz/1½ cups plain flour
10ml/2 tsp caster sugar
2 eggs
450ml/¾ pint/1¼ cups milk
25g/1oz/2 tbsp butter, melted

1 Sift the flour into a bowl and stir in the sugar. Make a well in the centre and add the eggs and half the milk. Stir, gradually incorporating the dry ingredients, until smooth, then beat in the remaining milk.

2 Stir most of the melted butter into the batter. Heat a pancake pan, then grease it lightly with butter. Spoon in about 60ml/4 tbsp of the batter, tilting the pan so it coats the bottom evenly. Cook until the pancake has set and small holes appear on the surface. Lift the edge; the base should be pale brown. Flip the pancake over. Cook the other side briefly. Slide out and keep hot while cooking more pancakes.

CHOCOLATE SAUCE

Preparation time 1 minute
Cooking time 5 minutes

MAKES 250ML/8FL OZ/1 CUP
150ml/¼ pint/⅔ cup single cream
15ml/1 tbsp caster sugar
*150g/5oz best quality plain
   chocolate, broken*
*30ml/2 tbsp dark rum or
   whisky (optional)*

1 Rinse out a small saucepan with cold water. This will help to prevent the sauce from catching on the bottom of the pan. Pour in the cream, stir in the sugar and bring to the boil over a medium heat.

2 Remove the pan from the heat and add the chocolate, a few pieces at a time, stirring after each addition until the chocolate has melted and the sauce is smooth. Stir in the rum or whisky, if using.

3 Pour the chocolate sauce into a jug and use immediately. Alternatively, pour the sauce into a clean jar and cool quickly. Close the jar and store the sauce in the fridge for up to 10 days. Serve hot or cold.

RASPBERRY PURÉE

Preparation time 1–2 minutes
Cooking time 1–5 minutes

1 Hull, clean and dry fresh raspberries and place them in a blender or food processor. Pulse the machine a few times, scraping down the sides of the bowl once or twice, until the berries form a purée.

2 If using frozen raspberries, put them in a saucepan with a little sugar and place over a gentle heat to soften and release the juices. Simmer for 5 minutes, then cool.

3 Press the purée through a fine-mesh sieve to remove any fibres or seeds. Sweeten with a little icing sugar and sharpen the flavour with lemon juice or a fruit-flavour liqueur, to taste.

COOK'S TIP
Other soft summer fruits can be used to make a purée, try strawberries or blueberries, which can be puréed raw, or peaches, apricots or nectarines, which should first be poached lightly.

MIX AND MATCH MENUS

You can produce an entire meal in less than half an hour if you mix and match carefully. Choose one dish that needs to stand or can be left to cook for at least ten minutes, during which time you can put together a starter, salad or speedy dessert. These flexible menus include recipes from the book and some simple ideas for which no recipe is needed.

TEENAGERS' TREAT

Guacamole can be made in moments and is delicious with either spicy tortilla chips or crisp vegetable dippers.

Save time and effort by getting each guest to top his or her own Pitta Pizza.

Instant salad: Mix bought ready-washed mixed salad leaves with sliced avocado, red onion, orange segments and walnuts.

Ice Cream Strawberry Shortcake is a quick and simple assembly job that is best done at the last minute.

FAMILY FAVOURITE

Fresh Tomato Soup needs to simmer for 10 minutes, during which time you can prepare the burgers and make the pudding.

Beef and Mushroom Burgers make a tasty main course. Sort out the salad while they cook.

Chopped salad vegetables with crumbled feta cheese and olives make Persian Salad a flavourful accompaniment. Add the dressing at the last moment

For a final flourish, serve Cornflake-topped Peach Bake with cream or vanilla ice cream.

SOPHISTICATED SUPPER

Sautéed Scallops are very quick and easy, so prepare them ahead if you like, but cook them at the very last minute.

Pan-fried Veal Chops is a good main course, make the sauce while cooking the starter.

As an accompaniment, serve crusty bread or rolls and Citrus Green Leaf Salad omitting the croûtons if time is very short.

There's no time to make an elaborate pudding, so simply serve fresh raspberries or strawberries and some clotted cream.

VEGETARIAN FEAST	PARTY TIME	LIGHT LUNCH

Make an easy appetizer by serving warm focaccia bread with sea salt crystals and olives.

Quick suggestions for party food: Serve Hummus with pitta bread instead of toast.

Melon and Grapefruit Cocktail is a cool and refreshing starter without being filling.

Leek and Caraway Gratin with a Carrot Crust can easily be baked alongside the tomatoes.

Tomato and Mozzarella Toasts resemble mini pizzas and a perfect for parties.

Crunchy-topped Cod is a good light main course, and needs very little attention during cooking.

Garlic Baked Tomatoes bring colour to the menu and taste absolutely delicious – if you like, substitute halved cherry tomatoes for the larger tomatoes and cut the cooking time by about half.

Finally, assemble Figs with Ricotta Cream while the main-course bakes are in the oven.

Smoked Mackerel and Apple Dip is another quick and easy starter. Serve it with crisp breadsticks, fingers of hot toast or colourful vegetable crudités.

Make miniature Asparagus Rolls and serve with the butter sauce or a ready-made mayonnaise dip.

While the cod is cooking, toss together Mixed Vegetables with Aromatic Seeds to serve as a tasty acccompaniment.

Brazilian Coffee Bananas is one of the easiest desserts in the book. Make it just before serving. Use nut-flavoured yogurt in place of the Greek yogurt, if you like.

10 MINUTE RECIPES

If you only have ten minutes to spare, take the fast track. Simple soups like Avgolemono get you off to a racing start, as do appetizers like Smoked Trout Salad or Parma Ham with Mango. Take a tip from the tapas table and try Garlic Prawns or Chorizo in Olive Oil. Want something substantial as well as speedy? Pork with Camembert fits the bill. Finally, as you roar into the home straight, Chocolate Fudge Sundaes or Brazilian Coffee Bananas will have everyone cheering.

AVGOLEMONO

This is the most popular of Greek soups. The name means egg and lemon, the two important ingredients, which produce a light, nourishing soup. Orzo is Greek, rice-shaped pasta, but you can use any small pasta shapes.

Preparation time 2 minutes
Cooking time 5 minutes

Serves 4–6
1.75 litres/3 pints/7½ cups chicken
   stock
115g/4oz/1 cup orzo pasta
3 eggs
juice of 1 large lemon
salt and ground black pepper
lemon slices, to garnish

1 Pour the stock into a large pan, and bring to the boil. Add the pasta and cook for 5 minutes.

2 Beat the eggs until frothy, then add the lemon juice and 15ml/ 1 tbsp of cold water. Slowly stir in a ladleful of the hot chicken stock, then add one or two more. Return this mixture to the pan, off the heat and stir well. Season with salt and pepper and serve at once, garnished with lemon slices. Do not let the soup boil once the eggs have been added or it will curdle.

Cook's Tips

Good-quality chicken stock is the secret of this speedy recipe. Look out for cartons of stock in the chilled cabinet of your local supermarket, or buy canned bouillon.

Making your own stock may sound like a chore, but if you recycle the meaty carcass of a roast chicken, it can be prepared in less time than it takes to clear the table after Sunday lunch.

Just pop the carcass in a pan, add an onion, a carrot and a bouquet garni, pour over water to cover generously and bring it to the boil. Lower the heat to the lowest setting, cover the pan and leave the stock to simmer for about 2 hours or until the aroma reminds you it is time to turn it off.

Strain the stock into a bowl, cool it quickly, then skim off any fat from the surface. Chicken stock freezes well for up to 3 months and should be seasoned on thawing.

Thai-Style Corn Soup

This is a very quick and easy soup. If you are using frozen prawns, thaw them before adding them to the soup.

Preparation time 3 minutes
Cooking time 5 minutes

Serves 4

2.5ml/ ½ tsp sesame or sunflower oil
2 spring onions, thinly sliced
1 garlic clove, crushed
600ml/1 pint/2½ cups chicken stock
425g/15oz can creamed corn
225g/8oz/1¼ cups cooked,
    peeled prawns
5ml/1 tsp green chilli paste or chilli
    sauce (optional)
salt and ground black pepper
fresh coriander leaves, to garnish

1 Heat the oil in a large heavy-based saucepan and sauté the spring onions and garlic over a medium heat, until softened.

2 Stir in the chicken stock, creamed corn, prawns and chilli paste or sauce, if using.

3 Bring the soup to the boil, stirring occasionally. Season with salt and ground black pepper to taste, then serve at once, sprinkling with fresh coriander leaves to garnish.

Cook's Tip
If creamed corn is not available, use ordinary canned sweetcorn, puréed in a food processor for a few seconds, until the mixture is creamy yet retains some texture.

Variations
To make Thai-style Crab and Corn Soup, use canned or freshly cooked crab in place of all or some of the cooked, peeled prawns.

PAN-FRIED CHICKEN LIVER SALAD

This Florentine salad uses vin santo, a delicious sweet dessert wine from Tuscany, but this is not essential — any dessert wine will do, or a sweet or cream sherry.

Preparation time 4 minutes
Cooking time 6 minutes

SERVES 4

75g/3oz fresh baby spinach leaves
75g/3oz lollo rosso leaves
75ml/5 tbsp olive oil
15g/ ½oz/1 tbsp butter
225g/8oz chicken livers, trimmed and thinly sliced
45ml/3 tbsp vin santo
50–75g/2–3oz fresh Parmesan cheese, shaved into curls
salt and ground black pepper

1 Wash and dry the spinach and lollo rosso. Tear the leaves into a large bowl, season with salt and ground black pepper to taste and toss gently to mix.

2 Heat 30ml/2 tbsp of the oil with the butter in a large heavy-based frying pan. When foaming, add the chicken livers and toss over a medium to high heat for 5 minutes or until the livers are browned on the outside but still pink in the centre. Remove from the heat.

3 Remove the livers from the pan with a slotted spoon, drain them on kitchen paper, then place on top of the salad leaves.

4 Return the pan to a medium heat, add the remaining oil and the vin santo and stir until sizzling. Pour the hot dressing over the leaves and livers and toss to coat. Put the salad in a serving bowl and sprinkle over the Parmesan shavings. Serve at once.

DEEP-FRIED WHITEBAIT

The spicy coating on these fish gives this fast favourite a crunchy bite.

Preparation time 2 minutes
Cooking time 7–8 minutes

SERVES 6

*115g/4oz/1 cup plain flour
2.5ml/ ½ tsp curry powder
2.5ml/ ½ tsp ground ginger
2.5ml/ ½ tsp ground cayenne pepper
pinch of salt
1.2kg/2 ½lb fresh or frozen
  whitebait, thawed
vegetable oil, for deep frying
lemon wedges, to garnish*

1 Sift the flour into a bowl and stir in the curry powder, ground ginger, cayenne and salt.

2 Lay two sheets of kitchen paper on the work surface. Spread out the whitebait on top, then cover with more kitchen paper. Blot the fish thoroughly to dry them.

3 Add a few whitebait at a time to the seasoned flour and stir gently until they are evenly coated. Heat the oil in a large, heavy-based saucepan until it reaches a temperature of 190°C/375°F.

4 Fry the whitebait in batches for 2–3 minutes until the fish is golden and crispy. Drain well on kitchen paper keeping each batch hot while cooking the next. Serve hot garnished with lemon wedges.

MELON AND GRAPEFRUIT COCKTAIL

This pretty, colourful starter is perfect for all those occasions when you don't have much time for cooking, but want something really special to eat.

Preparation time 8 minutes
Cooking time Nil

SERVES 4

1 small Galia or Ogen melon
1 small Charentais melon
2 pink grapefruit
45ml/3 tbsp orange juice
60ml/4 tbsp red vermouth
seeds from ½ pomegranate
mint sprigs, to garnish

COOK'S TIP
To check if the melons are ripe, smell them – they should have a heady aroma, and give slightly when pressed gently at the stalk end.

1 Halve the melons lengthways and scoop out all the seeds. Cut into wedges and remove the skins, then cut across into large bite-size pieces. Set the melon aside.

2 Using a small sharp knife, cut the peel and pith from the grapefruit. Holding the fruit over a bowl to catch the juice, cut between the grapefruit membranes to release the segments.

3 Stir the orange juice and vermouth into the reserved grapefruit juice.

4 Arrange the melon pieces and grapefruit segments on four individual serving plates. Spoon over the dressing, then scatter with the pomegranate seeds. Decorate with mint sprigs.

PARMA HAM WITH MANGO

Other fresh, colourful fruits, such as figs, papaya or melon would go equally well with the Parma ham in this light, elegant starter. It is amazingly simple to prepare and can be made in advance – ideal if you are serving a complicated main course.

Preparation time 5 minutes
Cooking time Nil

SERVES 4

12 slices Parma ham
1 ripe mango
ground black pepper
flat leaf parsley sprigs, to garnish

1 Separate the Parma ham slices and arrange three on each of four individual plates, crumpling the Parma ham slightly to give a decorative effect.

2 Cut the mango flesh off the stone, then slice and peel it.

3 Just before serving, arrange the mango slices in among the ham. Grind over some black pepper or offer this at the table. Garnish with flat leaf parsley sprigs.

CHORIZO IN OLIVE OIL

Spanish chorizo sausage has a deliciously pungent taste; its robust seasoning of garlic, chilli and paprika flavours the ingredients it is cooked with. Frying chorizo with onions and olive oil is one of its simplest and most delicious uses.

**Preparation time 2 minutes
Cooking time 7–8 minutes**

SERVES 4

*75ml/5 tbsp extra virgin olive oil
350g/12oz chorizo sausage, sliced
1 large onion, thinly sliced
roughly chopped flat leaf parsley,
   to garnish
warm bread, to serve*

1 Heat the oil in a frying pan and fry the chorizo slices over a high heat until they begin to colour. Lift out with a slotted spoon.

2 Add the onion to the pan and fry until coloured. Return the sausage slices to the pan and heat through for 1 minute.

3 Tip the mixture into a shallow serving dish and scatter with the parsley. Serve with warm bread.

VARIATION
Chorizo is usually available in large supermarkets or delicatessens. Other similarly rich, spicy sausages can be used as a substitute.

GARLIC PRAWNS

For this simple Spanish tapas dish, you really need fresh raw prawns that will absorb the flavours of the garlic and chilli as they fry. Have everything ready for last-minute cooking so that you can take it to the table still sizzling.

**Preparation time 5 minutes
Cooking time 5 minutes**

SERVES 4

*350–450g/12oz–1lb large raw prawns
2 red chillies
75ml/5 tbsp olive oil
3 garlic cloves, crushed
salt and ground black pepper*

1 Remove the heads and shells from the prawns, leaving the tails intact.

2 Halve each chilli lengthways and discard the seeds. Heat the oil in a flameproof pan, suitable for serving. (Alternatively, use a frying pan and have a warmed serving dish ready in the oven.)

3 Add all the prawns, chillies and garlic to the pan and cook over a high heat for about 3 minutes, stirring until the prawns turn pink. Season lightly with salt and pepper and serve immediately.

MELON, PINEAPPLE AND GRAPE COCKTAIL

A light fresh fruit salad, with no added sugar, makes a refreshing and speedy starter.

Preparation time 6 minutes
Cooking time Nil

SERVES 4

½ melon
225g/8oz fresh pineapple
225g/8oz seedless white grapes, halved
120ml/4fl oz/ ½ cup white grape juice
fresh mint leaves, to garnish

1 Remove the seeds from the melon half and use a melon baller to scoop out even-size balls.

2 Using a sharp knife, cut the skin from the pineapple. Cut the fruit into bite-size chunks.

3 Combine all the fruits in a glass serving dish and pour over the white grape juice. Serve immediately or cover and chill until required. Garnish with mint leaves.

COOK'S TIP
To save even more time, use a 225g/ 8oz can of pineapple chunks in natural juice. Drain the chunks, reserving the juice in a measuring jug. Make it up to the required quantity for pouring over the fruit with white grape juice.

SMOKED TROUT SALAD

Horseradish is as good a partner to smoked trout as it is to roast beef. In this recipe it is combined with yogurt to make a delicious light salad dressing.

Preparation time 6 minutes
Cooking time Nil

SERVES 4

1 oakleaf or other red lettuce
225g/8oz small tomatoes, cut into thin wedges
½ cucumber, peeled and thinly sliced
4 smoked trout fillets, about 200g/7oz each, skinned and flaked
For the dressing
pinch of English mustard powder
15–20ml/3–4 tsp white wine vinegar
30ml/2 tbsp light olive oil
100ml/3½fl oz/scant ½ cup natural yogurt
about 30ml/2 tbsp grated fresh or bottled horseradish
pinch of caster sugar

| 1 | First, make the dressing. Mix together the mustard powder and vinegar, then gradually whisk in the oil, yogurt, horseradish and sugar.

VARIATION
This salad is equally good with smoked mackerel. Add a garnish of lime or orange slices, slit to the centre and twisted.

| 2 | Place the lettuce leaves in a large bowl. Stir the dressing again, then pour half of it over the leaves and toss lightly.

| 3 | Arrange the lettuce on four individual plates with the tomatoes, cucumber and trout. Spoon over the remaining dressing and serve at once.

HOT TOMATO AND MOZZARELLA SALAD

A quick, easy starter with a Mediterranean flavour. It can be prepared in advance, chilled, then grilled just before serving.

Preparation time 5 minutes
Cooking time 4–5 minutes

SERVES 4

450g/1lb plum tomatoes, sliced
225g/8oz mozzarella cheese, sliced
1 red onion, finely chopped
4–6 pieces sun-dried tomatoes in oil, drained and chopped
60ml/4 tbsp olive oil
5ml/1 tsp red wine vinegar
2.5ml/ 1/2 tsp Dijon mustard
60ml/4 tbsp chopped fresh mixed herbs, such as basil, parsley, oregano and chives
salt and ground black pepper
fresh herb sprigs, to garnish

1 Arrange the sliced tomatoes and mozzarella in concentric circles in four individual shallow flameproof dishes.

2 Scatter over the chopped onion and sun-dried tomatoes. Preheat the grill to high.

3 Whisk together the olive oil, vinegar, mustard, chopped herbs and seasoning. Pour over the salads.

4 Place the salads under the hot grill for 4–5 minutes, until the mozzarella starts to melt. Grind over plenty of black pepper and serve immediately, garnished with fresh herb sprigs, if liked.

ASPARAGUS WITH TARRAGON BUTTER

Eating fresh asparagus with your fingers can be messy, but it is the only proper way to eat it!

Preparation time 2 minutes
Cooking time 6–8 minutes

SERVES 4

500g/1 1/4 lb fresh asparagus
115g/4oz/ 1/2 cup butter
30ml/2 tbsp chopped fresh tarragon
15ml/1 tbsp chopped fresh parsley, plus extra to garnish
grated rind of 1/2 lemon
15ml/1 tbsp lemon juice
salt and ground black pepper

COOK'S TIP
When buying fresh asparagus, choose spears that are plump and have a good even colour with tightly budded tips. The best asparagus is home-grown, as it starts to lose its flavour when cut.

1 Trim the woody ends from the asparagus spears, then tie them into four equal bundles.

2 Place the bundles of asparagus in a large frying pan with about 2.5cm/1in boiling water. Cover and cook for about 6–8 minutes, until the asparagus is tender but still firm. Drain well and discard the strings.

3 Meanwhile, melt the butter in a small pan. Add the tarragon, parsley, lemon rind and juice.

4 Arrange the asparagus spears on four warmed serving plates. Season the hot tarragon butter with salt and ground black pepper, pour it over the asparagus and serve at once. Garnish with more chopped parsley.

GUACAMOLE

Nachos or tortilla chips are the perfect accompaniment for this classic Mexican dip.

Preparation time 5 minutes
Cooking time Nil

SERVES 4
2 ripe avocados
2 red chillies, seeded
1 garlic clove
1 shallot
30ml/2 tbsp olive oil, plus extra to serve
juice of 1 lemon
salt
flat leaf parsley leaves, to garnish

1 Halve the avocados, remove their stones and, using a spoon, scoop out their flesh into a bowl.

2 Mash the flesh well with a large fork or a potato masher.

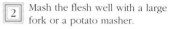

3 Finely chop the chillies, garlic and shallot, then stir into the mashed avocado with the olive oil and lemon juice. Add salt to taste.

4 Spoon the mixture into a small serving bowl. Drizzle over a little olive oil and scatter with a few flat leaf parsley leaves. Serve.

HUMMUS

Serve this nutritious dip with vegetable crudités for a simple and satisfying starter or spread it thickly on hot buttered toast.

Preparation time 5 minutes
Cooking time 2–3 minutes

SERVES 4
400g/14oz can chick-peas, drained
2 garlic cloves
30ml/2 tbsp tahini or unsweetened
    smooth peanut butter
60ml/4 tbsp olive oil
juice of 1 lemon
2.5ml/ ½ tsp cayenne pepper
15ml/1 tbsp sesame seeds
sea salt

1 Rinse the chick-peas well and place in a blender or food processor with the garlic and a good pinch of sea salt.

2 Add the tahini or peanut butter and process until fairly smooth. With the motor still running, slowly pour in the oil and lemon juice.

COOK'S TIP
Tahini is a thick, smooth and oily paste made from sesame seeds. It is available from health-food shops and large supermarkets. Tahini is a classic ingredient in hummus, this Middle-Eastern dip; peanut butter would not be used in a traditional recipe, but it is a useful substitute.

3 Stir in the cayenne pepper and add more salt, to taste. If the mixture is too thick, stir in a little cold water. Transfer the purée to a serving bowl.

4 Heat a small non-stick pan and add the sesame seeds. Cook for 2–3 minutes, shaking the pan, until the seeds are golden. Allow to cool, then sprinkle over the purée.

MELTING CHEESE DIP

This is a classic fondue in true Swiss style. It should be served with cubes of crusty, day-old bread, but it is also good with chunks of spicy, cured sausage such as chorizo.

Preparation time 3 minutes
Cooking time 7 minutes

SERVES 2

1 garlic clove, finely chopped
150ml/ ¼ pint/ ⅔ cup dry white wine
150g/5oz Gruyère cheese
5ml/1 tsp cornflour
15ml/1 tbsp Kirsch
salt and ground black pepper
bread or chorizo cubes, to serve

1 Place the garlic and wine in a small saucepan and bring gently to the boil. Lower the heat and simmer for 3–4 minutes.

COOK'S TIP
Gruyère is a tasty cheese that melts incredibly well. Don't substitute other cheeses in this dip.

2 Coarsely grate the cheese and stir it into the wine. Continue to stir as the cheese melts.

3 Blend the cornflour to a smooth paste with the Kirsch and pour into the pan, stirring. Bring to the boil, stirring continuously until the sauce is smooth and thickened.

4 Add salt and pepper to taste. Serve immediately in heated bowls or transfer to a fondue pan and keep hot over a spirit burner. Garnish with black pepper and serve with bread or chorizo cubes speared on fondue forks.

CIABATTA WITH MOZZARELLA AND GRILLED ONION

Ciabatta is readily available in most supermarkets. It's even more delicious when made with spinach, sun-dried tomatoes or olives, and you'll probably find these in your local delicatessen.

Preparation time 3 minutes
Cooking time 7 minutes

MAKES 4
1 ciabatta loaf
60ml/4 tbsp red pesto
2 small mild onions
oil, for brushing
225g/8oz mozzarella cheese
8 black olives

1 Preheat the grill to high. Cut the bread in half horizontally and toast lightly. Spread with the red pesto. Leave the grill on.

VARIATIONS
Toast halved baguettes and top with sliced cherry tomatoes and goat's cheese, then grill and garnish with shredded fresh basil.
    Toast halved French sticks, spread with passata and top with slices of mozzarella, anchovies and black olives, then grill and garnish with fresh oregano leaves.

2 Peel the onions and cut them horizontally into thick slices. Brush with oil and grill for 3 minutes until lightly browned.

3 Slice the cheese and arrange over the bread. Lay the onion slices on top and scatter some olives over. Cut in half diagonally. Place under a hot grill for 2–3 minutes until the cheese melts and the onion chars.

SALAD LEAVES WITH GORGONZOLA

Crispy fried pancetta makes a tasty addition and contrasts well in texture and flavour with the softness of mixed salad leaves and the sharp taste of Gorgonzola. If pancetta is not available, use unsmoked streaky bacon instead.

Preparation time 5 minutes
Cooking time 5 minutes

SERVES 4

225g/8oz pancetta rashers, any rinds removed, coarsely chopped
2 large garlic cloves, roughly chopped
75g/3oz rocket leaves
75g/3oz radicchio leaves
50g/2oz/ ½ cup walnuts, roughly chopped
115g/4oz Gorgonzola cheese
60ml/4 tbsp olive oil
15ml/1 tbsp balsamic vinegar
salt and ground black pepper

1 Put the chopped pancetta and garlic in a non-stick or heavy-based frying pan and heat gently, stirring constantly, until the pancetta fat runs. Increase the heat and fry until the pancetta and garlic are crisp. Try not to let the garlic brown or it will acquire a bitter flavour. Remove the pancetta and garlic with a slotted spoon and drain on kitchen paper. Leave the pancetta fat in the pan, off the heat.

2 Tear the rocket and radicchio leaves into a salad bowl. Sprinkle over the walnuts, pancetta and garlic. Add salt and pepper and toss to mix. Crumble the Gorgonzola on top.

3 Return the frying pan to a medium heat and add the oil and balsamic vinegar to the pancetta fat. Stir until sizzling, then pour over the salad. Serve at once, to be tossed at the table.

TOMATO AND MOZZARELLA TOASTS

These resemble mini pizzas and are good with drinks before a dinner party. If you prefer, you can prepare them several hours in advance and pop them in the oven just as your guests arrive.

Preparation time 3 minutes
Cooking time 7 minutes

SERVES 6–8

3 sfilatini (thin ciabatta)
about 250ml/8 fl oz/1 cup sun-dried tomato paste
3 x 150g/5oz packets mozzarella cheese, drained and chopped
about 10ml/2 tsp dried oregano or mixed herbs
30– 45ml/2–3 tbsp olive oil
ground black pepper

1 Preheat the oven to 220ºC/ 425ºF/Gas 7. Also preheat the grill. Cut each sfilatino on the diagonal into 12–15 slices, discarding the ends. Grill until lightly toasted on both sides. Spread sun-dried tomato paste on one side of each slice of toast. Arrange the mozzarella over the tomato paste.

2 Put the toasts on baking sheets, sprinkle with herbs and pepper to taste and drizzle with oil. Bake for 5 minutes or until the mozzarella has melted and is bubbling. Leave the toasts to settle for a few minutes before serving.

Cashew Chicken

In this Chinese-inspired dish, tender pieces of chicken are stir-fried with cashew nuts, red chillies and a touch of garlic.

Preparation time 4 minutes
Cooking time 6 minutes

Serves 4–6
450g/1lb boneless chicken breasts
30ml/2 tbsp vegetable oil
2 garlic cloves, sliced
4 dried red chillies, chopped
1 red pepper, seeded and diced
30ml/2 tbsp oyster sauce
15ml/1 tbsp soy sauce
1 bunch spring onions, cut into
   5cm/2in lengths
175g/6oz/1½ cups cashew nuts,
   roasted
coriander leaves, to garnish

1 Remove and discard the skin from the chicken breasts. With a sharp knife, cut the chicken into bite-size pieces and set aside.

2 Heat the oil in a wok and swirl it around. Add the garlic and dried chillies and fry until golden.

3 Add the chicken and stir-fry until it changes colour, then add the red pepper.

4 Stir in the oyster sauce and soy sauce. Add the spring onions and cashew nuts. Stir-fry for 1–2 minutes more. Serve garnished with coriander leaves.

STIR-FRIED CHICKEN WITH BASIL AND CHILLIES

This quick and easy chicken dish is an excellent introduction to Thai cuisine. Deep frying the basil adds another dimension to this dish. Thai basil, which is sometimes known as Holy basil, has a unique, pungent flavour that is both spicy and sharp. The dull leaves have serrated edges.

Preparation time 3 minutes
Cooking time 7 minutes

SERVES 4–6

45ml/3 tbsp vegetable oil
4 garlic cloves, sliced
2–4 red chillies, seeded and chopped
450g/1lb chicken, cut into bite-size pieces
30–45ml/2–3 tbsp fish sauce
10ml/2 tsp dark soy sauce
5ml/1 tsp sugar
10–12 Thai basil leaves
2 red chillies, sliced, to garnish
20 Thai basil leaves, deep fried (optional)

1 Heat the oil in a wok or large frying pan and swirl it around.

COOK'S TIP
To deep fry Thai basil leaves, make sure that the leaves are completely dry. Deep fry in hot oil for about 30–40 seconds, lift out using a slotted spoon and drain on kitchen paper.

2 Add the garlic and chillies and stir-fry until golden.

3 Add the chicken and stir-fry until it changes colour.

4 Season with fish sauce, soy sauce and sugar. Continue to stir-fry for 3–4 minutes or until the chicken is cooked. Stir in the fresh Thai basil leaves. Garnish with the chillies and the fried basil, if using.

Thai Chicken and Vegetable Stir-fry

Preparation time 3 minutes
Cooking time 7 minutes

Serves 4

1 lemon grass stalk
1cm/ ½ in piece of fresh root ginger
1 large garlic clove
30ml/2 tbsp sunflower oil
275g/10oz lean chicken, thinly sliced
½ red pepper, seeded and sliced
½ green pepper, seeded and sliced
4 spring onions, chopped
2 carrots, cut into matchsticks
115g/4oz fine green beans
30ml/2 tbsp oyster sauce
pinch of sugar
salt and ground black pepper
crushed peanuts and coriander
    leaves, to garnish

1. Thinly slice the lemon grass. Peel and chop the ginger and garlic. Heat the oil in a frying pan over a high heat. Add the lemon grass, ginger and garlic, and stir-fry for 30 seconds until the garlic is golden and the oil is aromatic.

2. Add the chicken and stir-fry for 2 minutes. Then add the vegetables; stir-fry for 3 minutes, until the chicken is cooked and the vegetables are crisp-tender.

3. Finally stir in the oyster sauce, sugar and seasoning to taste and stir-fry for another minute or two to mix and blend well. Serve at once, sprinkled with the peanuts and coriander leaves. Rice is the traditional accompaniment.

Cook's Tips
Make this quick supper dish a little hotter by adding more fresh root ginger, if you wish. If you can get hold of it, try fresh galangal instead of ginger. The flavour is similar, but has peppery overtones.

CHICKEN WITH TOMATOES AND OLIVES

Chicken breasts or turkey, veal or pork escalopes can be flattened for quick and even cooking. You can buy them ready-prepared in France, but they are easy to do at home.

Preparation time 5 minutes
Cooking time 5 minutes

SERVES 4

4 skinless boneless chicken breasts (about 150–175g/5–6oz each)
1.5ml/ ¼ tsp cayenne pepper
75–105ml/5–7 tbsp extra virgin olive oil
6 ripe plum tomatoes
1 garlic clove, finely chopped
16–24 stoned black olives
small handful of fresh basil leaves
salt

1 Carefully remove the fillets (the long finger-shaped muscle on the back of each breast) and reserve for another use.

COOK'S TIP
If the tomato skins are at all tough, remove them by cutting a cross in the base of each tomato with a knife, then plunging them into boiling water for about 45 seconds. The skin should simply peel off. If you have a gas cooker, you can achieve the same result by preparing the tomatoes in the same way, spearing each one in turn on a fork and rotating it in the open flame until the skin peels back.

2 Place each chicken breast between two sheets of greaseproof paper or clear film and pound with the flat side of a meat hammer or roll out with a rolling pin to flatten to about 1cm/½in thick. Season with the cayenne pepper.

3 Heat 45–60ml/3–4 tbsp of the olive oil in a large heavy-based frying pan over a medium-high heat. Add the flattened chicken breasts and cook for 3–4 minutes until golden brown and just cooked, turning them once. Transfer the chicken to warmed serving plates and season with a little salt. Keep the chicken hot.

4 Peel the tomatoes (see Cook's Tip), then seed and chop.

5 Wipe out the frying pan and return to the heat. Add another 30–45ml/2–3 tbsp of olive oil and fry the garlic for 1 minute until golden and fragrant. Stir in the olives, cook for a further 1 minute, then stir in the tomatoes. Shred the basil leaves and stir into the olive and tomato mixture, then spoon it over the chicken and serve at once.

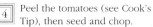

Turkey Escalopes with Capers

A staple of bistro cooking, these thin slices of poultry or meat, called escalopes or sometimes paillards, cook very quickly and can be served with all kinds of interesting sauces.

Preparation time 6 minutes
Cooking time 4 minutes

Serves 2

4 thin turkey breast escalopes (about 75g/3oz each)
1 large unwaxed lemon
2.5ml/ ½ tsp chopped fresh sage
60–75ml/4–5 tbsp extra virgin olive oil
50g/2oz/ ½ cup fine dry breadcrumbs
15ml/1 tbsp capers, rinsed and drained
salt and ground black pepper
sage leaves and lemon wedges, to garnish

1 Place the turkey escalopes between two sheets of greaseproof paper or clear film and pound with the flat side of a meat hammer or roll with a rolling pin to flatten to about a 5mm/¼ in thickness.

2 With a vegetable peeler, remove four pieces of lemon rind. Cut them into thin julienne strips, cover with clear film and set aside. Grate the remainder of the lemon rind and squeeze the lemon. Put the grated rind in a large shallow dish and add the sage, salt and pepper. Stir in 15ml/1 tbsp of the lemon juice, reserving the rest, and about 15ml/1 tbsp of the olive oil, then add the turkey, turn to coat and set aside.

3 Place the breadcrumbs in another shallow dish and dip the escalopes in the crumbs, coating both sides. In a heavy frying pan heat 30ml/2 tbsp of the olive oil over a high heat, add the escalopes and cook for 2–3 minutes, turning once, until golden. Transfer to two warmed plates and keep warm.

4 Wipe out the pan, add the remaining oil, the lemon julienne and the capers, stirring, and heat through. Spoon a little sauce over the turkey and garnish with sage leaves and lemon.

VEAL ESCALOPES WITH LEMON

Popular in Italian restaurants, this dish is very easy to make at home.

Preparation time 4 minutes
Cooking time 4 minutes

SERVES 4

4 veal escalopes
30–45 ml/2–3 tbsp plain flour
50g/2oz/¼ cup butter
60ml/4 tbsp olive oil
60ml/4 tbsp Italian dry white
  vermouth or dry white wine
45ml/3 tbsp lemon juice
salt and ground black pepper
lemon rind, lemon wedges and fresh
  parsley, to garnish
green beans and peperonata, to serve

1. Put each escalope between two sheets of greaseproof paper or clear film and pound until very thin. Cut the pounded escalopes in half or quarters, and coat in the flour, seasoned with salt and pepper.

COOK'S TIP
To make the peperonata suggested as an accompaniment, heat 75ml/5 tbsp olive oil in a pan, add 1 chopped onion, 2 diced red peppers, 1 crushed garlic clove and 2 chopped tomatoes and cook gently for 15 minutes. Serve hot or cold.

2. Melt the butter with half the oil in a large, heavy frying pan until sizzling. Add as many escalopes as the pan will hold. Fry over a medium to high heat for 1–2 minutes on each side until lightly coloured. Remove with a fish slice and keep hot. Add the remaining oil and cook the remaining veal escalopes in the same way.

3. Remove the pan from the heat and add the vermouth or wine and the lemon juice. Stir vigorously to mix with the pan juices, then return the pan to the heat and return all the veal to the pan. Spoon the sauce over the escalopes. Shake the pan over a medium heat until all of the escalopes are coated in the sauce and heated through.

4. Serve at once, garnished with lemon rind, lemon wedges and parsley. Lightly cooked green beans and peperonata make a delicious accompaniment.

VARIATION
Use skinless boneless chicken breasts instead of the veal. If they are thick, cut them in half before pounding.

PAN-FRIED VEAL CHOPS

*Veal chops from the loin are an
expensive cut and are best cooked
quickly and simply. The flavour of
basil goes well with veal, but you
could use another herb, such as
rosemary or parsley.*

Preparation time 2 minutes
Cooking time 7–8 minutes

SERVES 2
25g/1oz/2 tbsp butter, softened
15ml/1 tbsp Dijon mustard
15ml/1 tbsp chopped fresh basil
olive oil, for brushing
2 veal loin chops, 2.5cm/1in thick
(about 225g/8oz each)
ground black pepper
fresh basil sprigs, to garnish

|1| To make the basil butter, cream the butter with the mustard and chopped basil in a small bowl, then season with pepper.

|2| Lightly oil a heavy frying pan or griddle. Set over a high heat until very hot but not smoking. Brush both sides of each chop with a little oil and season with a little pepper.

|3| Place the chops on the pan or griddle and reduce the heat to medium. Cook for 4–5 minutes, then turn and cook for 3–4 minutes more until done as preferred (medium-rare meat will still be slightly soft when pressed, medium meat will be springy and well-done firm). Top each chop with half the basil butter and serve, garnished with basil.

VEAL ESCALOPES WITH TARRAGON

*These thin slices of veal need little
cooking, and the sauce is made very
quickly as well.*

Preparation time 4 minutes
Cooking time 6 minutes

SERVES 4
4 veal escalopes (about
115–150g/4–5oz each)
15g/ 1/2oz/1 tbsp butter
30ml/2 tbsp brandy
250ml/8fl oz/1 cup chicken or
beef stock
15ml/1 tbsp chopped fresh tarragon
salt and ground black pepper
fresh tarragon sprigs, to garnish

|1| Place the veal escalopes between two sheets of greaseproof paper or clear film and pound with the flat side of a meat mallet or roll them with a rolling pin to flatten to about 5mm/¼in thickness. Season with salt and ground black pepper.

|2| Melt the butter in a large frying pan over a medium-high heat. Add enough meat to the pan to fit easily in one layer (do not overcrowd the pan, cook in batches if necessary) and cook for 1½–2 minutes, turning once. Each escalope should be lightly browned, but must not be overcooked. Transfer to a platter and cover to keep warm.

|3| Add the brandy to the pan, then pour in the stock and bring to the boil. Add the tarragon and continue boiling until the liquid is reduced by half.

|4| Return the veal to the pan with any accumulated juices and heat through. Serve immediately, garnished with tarragon sprigs.

CALF'S LIVER WITH HONEY

Liver is the perfect choice for a quick meal. Although it can be braised, it is at its best when simply flashed in a hot pan. Cook the liver until it is browned on the outside but still rosy pink in the centre.

Preparation time 2 minutes
Cooking time 4–5 minutes

SERVES 4

4 slices calf's liver (about 175g/6oz
   each and 1cm/½in thick)
plain flour, for dusting
25g/1oz/2 tbsp butter
30ml/2 tbsp vegetable oil
30ml/2 tbsp sherry vinegar or red
   wine vinegar
30–45ml/2–3 tbsp chicken stock
15ml/1 tbsp clear honey
salt and ground black pepper
watercress sprigs, to garnish

1 Wipe the liver slices with damp kitchen paper, then season both sides with a little salt and pepper and dust the slices lightly with flour, shaking off any excess.

COOK'S TIP
It is important to use calf's liver, as it is tender and delicately flavoured. You could get away with lamb's liver, but don't use any other type.

2 In a large heavy frying pan, melt half of the butter with the oil over a high heat and swirl to blend thoroughly.

3 Add the liver slices to the pan and cook for 1–2 minutes until browned on one side, then turn and cook for a further 1 minute. Transfer to warmed plates and keep warm.

4 Stir the vinegar, stock and honey into the pan. Boil for about 1 minute, stirring constantly, then add the remaining butter, stirring until melted and smooth. Spoon over the liver slices and garnish with watercress sprigs.

PORK IN SWEET-AND-SOUR SAUCE

The combination of sweet-and-sour flavours is popular in Venetian cooking, especially with meat and liver. This recipe is given extra bite with the addition of crushed mixed peppercorns. Served with shelled broad beans tossed with grilled bacon, it is delectable.

Preparation time 2–3 minutes
Cooking time 6 minutes

SERVES 2
1 whole pork fillet, about 350g/12oz
25ml/1½ tbsp plain flour
30–45ml/2–3 tbsp olive oil
250ml/8fl oz/1 cup dry white wine
30ml/2 tbsp white wine vinegar
10ml/2 tsp granulated sugar
15ml/1 tbsp mixed peppercorns,
  coarsely ground
salt and ground black pepper
cooked broad beans tossed with
  grilled bacon, to serve

1 Cut the pork diagonally into thin slices. Place between two sheets of clear film and pound lightly with a rolling pin to flatten them.

2 Spread out the flour in a shallow bowl. Season well and coat the meat. Alternatively, put the seasoned flour in a strong plastic bag, add the pork and shake to coat.

3 Heat 15ml/1 tbsp of the oil in a wide heavy-based saucepan or frying pan and add as many slices of pork as the pan will hold. Fry over a medium to high heat for 2–3 minutes on each side until crisp and tender. Remove with a fish slice and set aside. Repeat with the remaining pork, adding more oil as necessary.

4 Mix the wine, vinegar and sugar in a jug. Pour into the pan and stir over a high heat until reduced. Stir in the peppercorns and return the pork to the pan. Spoon the sauce over the pork until it is evenly coated and heated through. Serve with cooked broad beans tossed with grilled bacon.

PORK WITH CAMEMBERT

When it comes to speedy feasts, pork fillet is an excellent choice. Beautifully tender, it needs very little cooking and is delicious served with a creamy cheese sauce.

Preparation time 2 minutes
Cooking time 7–8 minutes

SERVES 3–4

350–450g/12oz–1lb pork fillet
15g/ ½oz/1 tbsp butter
45ml/3 tbsp sparkling dry cider or dry white wine
120–175ml/4–6fl oz/ ½–¾ cup crème fraîche or whipping cream
15ml/1 tbsp chopped fresh mixed herbs, such as marjoram, thyme and sage
½ Camembert cheese (115g/4oz), rind removed (65g/2½oz without rind), sliced
7.5ml/1½ tsp Dijon mustard
ground black pepper
fresh parsley, to garnish

1 Slice the pork fillet crossways into small steaks about 2cm/¾in thick. Place between two sheets of greaseproof paper or clear film and pound with the flat side of a meat mallet or roll with a rolling pin to flatten to a thickness of 1cm/½in. Sprinkle with pepper.

VARIATION
Any creamy cheese that is not too soft can be used instead of Camembert. Try Cambazola or Brie for a change.

2 Melt the butter in a heavy frying pan over a medium-high heat until it begins to brown, then add the meat. Cook for 5 minutes, turning once, or until just cooked through and the meat is springy when pressed. Transfer to a warmed dish and cover to keep warm.

3 Add the cider or wine and bring to the boil, scraping the base of the pan. Stir in the cream and herbs and bring back to the boil.

4 Add the cheese and mustard and any accumulated juices from the meat. Stir until the cheese melts. Add a little more cream if needed and adjust the seasoning. Serve the pork with the sauce and garnish with parsley.

SALMON WITH GREEN PEPPERCORNS

A fashionable discovery of nouvelle cuisine, green peppercorns add piquancy to all kinds of sauces and stews. Available pickled in jars or cans, they are great to keep on hand in your store cupboard.

**Preparation time 1 minute
Cooking time 9 minutes**

SERVES 4

15g/ ½oz/1 tbsp butter
2 or 3 shallots, finely chopped
15ml/1 tbsp brandy (optional)
60ml/4 tbsp dry white wine
90ml/6 tbsp fish or chicken stock
120ml/4fl oz/ ½ cup whipping cream
30–45ml/2–3 tbsp green peppercorns
  in brine, rinsed and drained
15–30ml/1–2 tbsp vegetable oil
4 pieces salmon fillet (175–200g/
  6–7oz each)
salt and ground black pepper
fresh parsley, to garnish

1 Melt the butter in a heavy saucepan over a medium heat. Add the shallots and cook for 1 minute until just softened.

2 Add the brandy, if using, and the white wine. Stir well, then pour in the stock and bring to the boil. Continue to boil hard until the liquid has reduced by three-quarters, stirring occasionally.

3 Reduce the heat, then add the cream and half the green peppercorns, crushing them slightly with the back of a spoon. Cook very gently for 4 minutes until the sauce is slightly thickened, then strain and stir in the remaining peppercorns. Keep the sauce warm over a very low heat, stirring occasionally, while you cook the salmon.

4 In a large heavy frying pan, heat the oil over a medium-high heat until very hot. Lightly season the salmon and cook for 3–4 minutes or until the flesh is opaque and flakes easily when tested with the tip of a sharp knife. Arrange the fish on warmed plates and pour over the sauce. Garnish with parsley.

HALIBUT WITH TOMATO VINAIGRETTE

Sauce vièrge, a lightly cooked mixture of tomatoes, aromatic fresh herbs and olive oil, can either be served at room temperature or, as in this dish, slightly warm.

Preparation time 4 minutes
Cooking time 5–6 minutes

SERVES 2

*3 large ripe beefsteak tomatoes,
  peeled, seeded and chopped
2 shallots or 1 small red onion,
  finely chopped
1 garlic clove, crushed
90ml/6 tbsp chopped mixed fresh
  herbs, such as parsley, coriander,
  basil, tarragon, chervil or chives
120ml/4fl oz/ ½ cup extra virgin
  olive oil, plus extra for greasing
4 halibut fillets or steaks
  (175–200g/6–7oz each)
salt and ground black pepper
green salad, to serve*

1 In a saucepan, mix together the tomatoes, shallots or onion, garlic and herbs. Stir in the oil and season with salt and ground black pepper. Cover the pan and leave the sauce to stand at room temperature while you grill the fish.

2 Preheat the grill. Line a grill pan with foil and brush the foil lightly with oil.

> COOK'S TIP
> If time permits, leave the sauce to stand for up to an hour.

3 Season the fish with salt and pepper. Place the fish on the foil and brush with a little extra oil. Grill for 5–6 minutes until the flesh is opaque and the top lightly browned.

4 Meanwhile, heat the sauce gently for a few minutes. Serve the fish with the sauce and a salad.

PAN-FRIED SOLE WITH LEMON BUTTER SAUCE

The delicate flavour and texture of sole is brought out in this simple, classic recipe. Lemon sole is used here because it is often easier to obtain — and less expensive — than Dover sole.

Preparation time 1 minute
Cooking time 9 minutes

SERVES 2

30–45ml/2–3 tbsp plain flour
4 lemon sole fillets
45ml/3 tbsp olive oil
50g/2oz/ ¼ cup butter
60ml/4 tbsp lemon juice
30ml/2 tbsp rinsed bottled capers
salt and ground black pepper
fresh flat leaf parsley and lemon
   wedges, to garnish

1 Season the flour with salt and black pepper. Coat the sole fillets evenly on both sides. Heat the oil with half the butter in a large shallow pan until foaming. Add two sole fillets and fry over a medium heat for 2–3 minutes on each side.

2 Lift out the sole fillets with a fish slice and place on a warmed serving platter. Keep hot. Fry the remaining sole fillets in the same way, then lift them out carefully and add them to the platter.

3 Remove the pan from the heat and add the lemon juice and remaining butter. Return the pan to a high heat and stir vigorously until the pan juices are sizzling and beginning to turn golden brown. Remove from the heat and stir in the capers.

4 Pour the pan juices over the sole, sprinkle with salt and pepper to taste and garnish with the parsley. Add the lemon wedges and serve at once.

COOK'S TIPS
It is important to cook the pan juices to the right colour after removing the fish. Too pale, and they will taste insipid, too dark, and they may taste bitter. Take great care not to be distracted at this point so that you can watch the colour of the juices change to a golden brown. If you don't like the flavour of capers, leave them out since the butter sauce is quite good enough to serve on its own.

PRAWN AND VEGETABLE BALTI

A delicious accompaniment to other Balti dishes. Double the quantities if serving it solo.

Preparation time 3 minutes
Cooking time 7 minutes

SERVES 4

175g/6oz cooked, peeled prawns, thawed if frozen
30ml/2 tbsp corn oil
1.5ml/ ¼ tsp onion seeds
4–6 curry leaves
115g/4oz/1 cup frozen peas
115g/4oz/ ⅔ cup frozen sweetcorn
1 large courgette, sliced
1 red pepper, seeded and roughly diced
5ml/1 tsp crushed coriander seeds
5ml/1 tsp crushed dried red chillies
15ml/1 tbsp lemon juice
salt
15ml/1 tbsp fresh coriander leaves, to garnish

1 Drain any excess liquid from the prawns and pat them dry on kitchen paper. Heat the oil with the onion seeds and curry leaves in a non-stick wok or frying pan.

COOK'S TIP
The best way to crush whole seeds is to use an electric spice grinder or a small marble pestle and mortar.

2 Add the prawns to the wok or frying pan and stir-fry until any liquid has evaporated.

3 Add the peas, sweetcorn, courgette and red pepper and stir-fry for 3–5 minutes more.

4 Add the coriander seeds, dried red chillies and lemon juice. Toss over the heat for 1 minute, season to taste and serve, garnished with the fresh coriander leaves.

GREEN PRAWN CURRY

A popular fragrant creamy curry that takes very little time to prepare. It can also be made with thin strips of chicken.

Preparation time 2 minutes
Cooking time 8 minutes

Serves 4–6
30ml/2 tbsp vegetable oil
30ml/2 tbsp green curry paste
450g/1lb raw king prawns, shelled
   and deveined
4 kaffir lime leaves, torn
1 lemon grass stalk, bruised
   and chopped
250ml/8fl oz/1 cup coconut milk
30ml/2 tbsp fish sauce
½ cucumber, seeded and cut into
   thin batons
10–15 basil leaves
sliced green chillies, to garnish

1   Heat the oil in a frying pan. Add the green curry paste and fry until bubbling and fragrant.

2   Add the prawns, lime leaves and lemon grass. Fry for about 2 minutes, until the prawns are pink.

3   Stir in the coconut milk and bring to a gentle boil. Simmer, stirring, for about 5 minutes or until the prawns are tender.

4   Stir in the fish sauce and cucumber. Tear the basil leaves and add them too, then top with the green chillies and serve.

SAUTÉED SCALLOPS

Scallops go well with all sorts of sauces, but simple cooking is the best way to enjoy their delicate, fresh-from-the-sea flavour.

Preparation time 1 minute
Cooking time 5 minutes

SERVES 2
450g/1lb shelled scallops
25g/1oz/2 tbsp butter
30ml/2 tbsp dry white vermouth
15ml/1 tbsp finely chopped
 fresh parsley
salt and ground black pepper

1 Rinse the scallops under cold running water to remove any sand or grit. Drain them well and pat dry using kitchen paper. Spread them out and season them lightly with salt and pepper.

2 In a frying pan large enough to hold the scallops in one layer, heat half the butter until it begins to colour. Sauté the scallops for 3–5 minutes, turning, until golden brown on both sides and just firm to the touch. Remove to a serving platter and cover to keep hot.

3 Add the vermouth to the hot frying pan, swirl in the remaining butter, stir in the parsley and pour the sauce over the scallops. Serve immediately.

GARLICKY SCALLOPS AND PRAWNS

Scallops and prawns provide a healthy meal in next to no time. This method of cooking comes from France and is popular in Provence.

Preparation time 1 minute
Cooking time 4–5 minutes

SERVES 2–4
6 large shelled scallops
6–8 large raw prawns, peeled
plain flour, for dusting
30–45ml/2–3 tbsp olive oil
1 garlic clove, finely chopped
15ml/1 tbsp chopped fresh basil
30–45ml/2–3 tbsp lemon juice
salt and ground black pepper

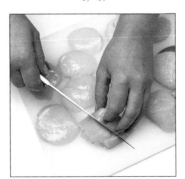

1 Rinse the scallops under cold running water to remove any sand or grit. Drain, then pat dry using kitchen paper. Cut them in half crossways. Season the scallops and prawns with salt and pepper and dust lightly with flour. Heat the oil in a large frying pan over a high heat and add the scallops and prawns.

2 Reduce the heat slightly and cook for 2 minutes, then turn the scallops and prawns and add the garlic and basil, shaking the pan to distribute them evenly. Cook for a further 2 minutes until the scallops are golden and just firm to the touch. Sprinkle over the lemon juice and toss to blend. Serve at once.

NOODLES WITH PINEAPPLE, GINGER AND CHILLIES

Preparation and
cooking time 8–10 minutes

SERVES 4

275g/10oz dried noodles
4 fresh or drained, canned
  pineapple rings
45ml/3 tbsp soft light brown sugar
60ml/4 tbsp fresh lime juice
60ml/4 tbsp coconut milk
30ml/2 tbsp fish sauce
30ml/2 tbsp grated fresh root ginger
2 garlic cloves, finely chopped
1 ripe mango or 2 peaches,
  finely diced
For the garnish
2 spring onions, sliced
2 red chillies, shredded
fresh mint leaves

1 Cook the noodles in a large
saucepan of boiling water until
tender, following the directions on
the packet.

2 Meanwhile, place the pineapple
rings on a flameproof dish,
sprinkle with 30ml/2 tbsp of the
sugar and grill until golden. Cut into
small dice.

3 Mix the lime juice, coconut
milk and fish sauce in a salad
bowl. Add the remaining brown sugar,
with the ginger and garlic, and whisk
well. Drain the noodles, refresh under
cold water and drain again. Add to the
bowl with the noodles and pineapple.

4 Add the mango or peaches and
toss lightly. Scatter the spring
onions, chillies and mint over. Serve.

BUCKWHEAT NOODLES WITH SMOKED SALMON

*Young pea sprouts are only
available for a short time. You can
substitute watercress, mustard cress,
young leeks or your favourite green
vegetable or herb in this dish.*

Preparation and
cooking time 8–10 minutes

SERVES 4

225g/8oz buckwheat or soba noodles
15ml/1 tbsp oyster sauce
juice of ½ lemon
30–45ml/2–3 tbsp light olive oil
115g/4oz smoked salmon, cut into
  fine strips
115g/4oz young pea sprouts
2 ripe tomatoes, peeled, seeded and
  cut into strips
15ml/1 tbsp snipped chives
salt and ground black pepper

1 Cook the buckwheat or soba
noodles in a large saucepan of
boiling water, following the
directions on the packet. Drain, then
tip into a colander and rinse under
cold running water. Drain well,
shaking the colander to extract any
remaining water.

2 Tip the noodles into a large
bowl. Add the oyster sauce and
lemon juice and season with pepper
to taste. Moisten with the olive oil.

3 Add the smoked salmon, pea
sprouts, tomatoes and chives.
Mix well and serve at once.

TAGLIATELLE WITH PROSCIUTTO AND ASPARAGUS

A stunning dish, this is very easy to make. Serve it for a special occasion.

Preparation and
cooking time 7–10 minutes

SERVES 4

350g/12oz fresh or dried tagliatelle
25g/1oz/2 tbsp butter
15ml/1 tbsp olive oil
225g/8oz asparagus tips
1 garlic clove, chopped
115g/4oz prosciutto, sliced
    into strips
30ml/2 tbsp chopped fresh sage
150ml/ ¼ pint/ ⅔ cup single cream
115g/4oz Double Gloucester
    cheese, grated
115g/4oz Gruyère cheese, grated
fresh sage leaves, to garnish

1 | Cook the pasta in a large saucepan of boiling water until tender, following the instructions on the packet.

2 | Meanwhile, melt the butter and oil in a frying pan and gently fry the asparagus tips for 3–4 minutes, or until almost tender.

3 | Stir in the garlic and prosciutto and fry for 1 minute.

4 | Stir in the sage leaves and fry for a further 1 minute, then pour in the cream. Bring to the boil over a medium heat, stirring frequently.

5 | Tip in the grated Double Gloucester and Gruyère cheeses. Simmer gently, stirring occasionally until thoroughly melted. Season to taste. Drain the pasta thoroughly and tip it into a bowl. Add the sauce and toss to coat. Serve immediately, garnished with fresh sage.

RAVIOLI WITH FOUR-CHEESE SAUCE

This has a smooth cheesy sauce that coats the pasta very evenly.

Preparation and
cooking time 5–6 minutes

SERVES 4

350g/12oz fresh ravioli
50g/2oz/ ¼ cup butter
50g/2oz/ ½ cup plain flour
450ml/ ¾ pint/scant 2 cups milk
50g/2oz Parmesan cheese
50g/2oz Edam cheese
50g/2oz Gruyère cheese
50g/2oz Fontina cheese
salt and ground black pepper
chopped fresh flat leaf parsley,
*   to garnish*

 Cook the pasta following the instructions on the packet.

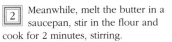 Meanwhile, melt the butter in a saucepan, stir in the flour and cook for 2 minutes, stirring.

3 Gradually stir in the milk until well blended.

4 Bring the milk to the boil over a low heat, stirring constantly until thickened.

5 Grate the cheeses and stir them into the sauce. Stir until they are just beginning to melt. Remove the sauce from the heat and season with salt and pepper.

6 Drain the pasta thoroughly and turn it into a large serving bowl. Pour over the sauce and toss to coat. Serve immediately, garnished with the chopped fresh parsley.

COOK'S TIP

If you cannot find all of the above cheeses, simply substitute your favourites. The aim is to have a total quantity of 225g/8oz cheese and to include Parmesan in the selection. Always buy Parmesan in the piece and grate it yourself – using the ready-grated cheese may save time, but the flavour will not be as good.

SPAGHETTI ALLA CARBONARA

This is a classic pasta dish. If you use fresh spaghetti, cook it at the last minute as it takes very little time.

Preparation and cooking time 7–10 minutes

SERVES 4

350g/12oz spaghetti
15ml/1 tbsp olive oil
1 onion, chopped
115g/4oz streaky bacon, rinded and diced, or pancetta
1 garlic clove, chopped
3 eggs
300ml/ ½ pint/1¼ cups double cream
50g/2oz Parmesan cheese
salt and ground black pepper
chopped fresh basil, to garnish

1. Cook the pasta following the instructions on the packet.

2. Meanwhile, heat the oil in a frying pan and fry the onion and bacon for 5 minutes until softened. Stir in the garlic and fry for a further 2 minutes, stirring.

3. Meanwhile, beat the eggs in a bowl, then stir in the cream and season with salt and pepper. Grate the Parmesan cheese and stir it into the cream mixture.

4. Stir the cream mixture into the onion and bacon and cook over a low heat for a few minutes, stirring constantly until heated through. Season to taste.

5. Drain the pasta thoroughly and turn it into a large serving bowl. Pour over the sauce and toss to coat. Serve immediately, garnished with chopped fresh basil.

COOK'S TIPS

Italians would use pancetta that is lightly cured but similar to streaky bacon. You can buy it in most supermarkets and delicatessens. If you use bacon, look out for packs of chopped streaky – a real time-saver.

SPINACH TAGLIARINI WITH ASPARAGUS

Fresh pasta is a boon to the busy cook. You may not be able to locate spinach tagliarini but any fresh pasta will work just as well.

Preparation time 2–4 minutes
Cooking time 6–8 minutes

SERVES 4–6

2 skinless, boneless chicken breasts
15ml/1 tbsp light soy sauce
30ml/2 tbsp sherry
30ml/2 tbsp cornflour
8 spring onions, cut into 2.5cm/1in
    diagonal slices
1–2 garlic cloves, crushed
needle shreds of rind of ½ lemon
150ml/¼ pint/⅔ cup chicken stock
5ml/1 tsp caster sugar
30ml/2 tbsp lemon juice
225g/8oz slender asparagus spears,
    cut in 7.5cm/3in lengths
450g/1lb fresh spinach tagliarini or
    other fresh pasta
salt and ground black pepper

1 Place the chicken breasts between two sheets of clear film and flatten to a thickness of 5mm/¼in with a rolling-pin. Using a sharp knife, cut the chicken into 2.5cm/1in strips across the grain. Put the chicken into a bowl with the soy sauce, sherry, cornflour and seasoning. Toss to coat each piece.

COOK'S TIP
Fresh pasta is ready as soon as it rises to the surface of the boiling water.

2 In a large non-stick frying pan, put the chicken, spring onions, garlic and needle shreds of lemon rind. Add the stock and bring to the boil, stirring constantly until thickened. Add the sugar, lemon juice and asparagus. Simmer for 4–5 minutes until tender.

3 Meanwhile, cook the pasta in a large pan of boiling salted water for 2–3 minutes until just tender. Drain thoroughly. Arrange on serving plates and spoon over the chicken and asparagus sauce. Serve the dish immediately.

FRENCH GOAT'S CHEESE SALAD

Preparation time 2–3 minutes
Cooking time 6 minutes

SERVES 4
200g/7oz bag prepared mixed
  salad leaves
4 rashers back bacon
115g/4oz full fat goat's cheese
16 thin slices French bread
For the dressing
60ml/4 tbsp olive oil
15ml/1 tbsp tarragon vinegar
10ml/2 tsp walnut oil
5ml/1 tsp Dijon mustard
5ml/1 tsp wholegrain mustard
salt and ground black pepper

1 Preheat the grill to a medium heat. Rinse and dry the salad leaves, then arrange in four individual bowls. Place the ingredients for the dressing in a screw-topped jar, shake together well and reserve.

2 Lay the bacon rashers on a board, then stretch with the back of a knife and cut each into four. Roll each piece up and grill for about 2–3 minutes.

3 Meanwhile, slice the goat's cheese into eight and halve each slice. Top each slice of bread with a piece of goat's cheese and pop under the grill. Turn over the bacon and continue cooking with the goat's cheese toasts until the cheese is golden and bubbling.

4 Arrange the bacon rolls and toasts on top of the prepared salad leaves. Shake the dressing well and pour a little of the dressing over each salad. Serve at once.

VARIATION
If you prefer, just slice the goat's cheese and place on toasted French bread. Or use wholewheat toast for a nutty flavour.

GREEK SALAD PITTAS

Horiatiki is the Greek name for this classic salad made with feta – a ewe's milk cheese. It is great in hot pitta breads.

Preparation time 5 minutes
Cooking time 2 minutes

MAKES 4
115g/4oz/1 cup diced feta cheese
¼ cucumber, peeled and diced
8 cherry tomatoes, quartered
½ small green pepper, seeded and
  thinly sliced
¼ small onion, thinly sliced
8 black olives, stoned and halved
30ml/2 tbsp olive oil
5ml/1 tsp dried oregano
4 large pitta breads
60ml/4 tbsp natural yogurt
5ml/1 tsp dried mint
salt and ground black pepper
fresh mint, to garnish

1 Place the cheese, cucumber, tomatoes, pepper, onion and olives in a bowl. Stir in the olive oil and oregano, then season well and set the bowl aside.

2 Place the pitta breads in a toaster or under a preheated grill for about 2 minutes, until puffed up. Meanwhile, to make the dressing, mix the yogurt with the mint, season well and reserve.

3 Holding the hot pittas in a tea towel, slice each one from top to bottom down one of the longer sides and open out to form a pocket.

4 Divide the prepared salad among the pitta bread pockets and drizzle over a spoonful of the yogurt dressing. Serve the filled pittas immediately, garnished with fresh mint. Offer the remaining dressing separately.

SPINACH SALAD WITH BACON AND PRAWNS

Preparation time 4 minutes
Cooking time 6 minutes

Serves 4
105ml/7 tbsp olive oil
30ml/2 tbsp sherry vinegar
2 garlic cloves, finely chopped
5ml/1 tsp Dijon mustard
12 cooked king prawns
115g/4oz rindless streaky bacon,
* cut into strips*
about 115g/4oz fresh young
* spinach leaves*
½ head oakleaf lettuce, roughly torn
salt and ground black pepper

1 To make the dressing, whisk together 90ml/6 tbsp of the olive oil with the vinegar, garlic, mustard and seasoning in a small pan. Heat gently until thickened slightly, then keep warm.

2 Carefully peel the prawns, leaving the tails intact.

3 Heat the remaining oil in a frying pan and fry the bacon until golden and crisp, stirring occasionally. Add the prawns and stir-fry until warmed through.

4 Trim the spinach leaves and arrange them with the torn oakleaf lettuce leaves on four individual serving plates.

5 Spoon the bacon and prawns on to the leaves, then pour over the hot dressing. Serve at once.

COOK'S TIP
Sherry vinegar lends its pungent flavour to this delicious salad. You can buy it from large supermarkets and good delicatessens.

CAESAR SALAD

For this famous salad, created in the 1920s by the Tijuanan chef called Caesar Cardini, the dressing is traditionally tossed into crunchy cos lettuce, but any crisp lettuce will do.

Preparation time 2 minutes
Cooking time 6–8 minutes

SERVES 4

1 large cos lettuce
4 thick slices white or Granary bread
    without crusts, cubed
45ml/3 tbsp olive oil
1 garlic clove, crushed
25g/1oz Parmesan cheese, grated
For the dressing
1 egg
1 garlic clove, chopped
30ml/2 tbsp lemon juice
dash of Worcestershire sauce
3 anchovy fillets, chopped
120ml/4fl oz/ ¹/₂ cup olive oil
salt and ground black pepper

1 Preheat the oven to 220°C/ 425°F/Gas 7. Separate, rinse and dry the lettuce leaves. Tear the outer leaves roughly and chop the heart roughly.

2 Arrange the lettuce in a salad bowl. Mix together the cubed bread, olive oil and garlic in a separate bowl. Leave for 2 minutes, until the bread has soaked up the flavoured oil. Lay the bread cubes on a baking sheet and place in the oven for about 6–8 minutes (keeping an eye on them) until golden brown.

3 Meanwhile, make the dressing. Break the egg in a food processor or blender and add the garlic, lemon juice, Worcestershire sauce and one of the anchovy fillets.

4 Blend the mixture until smooth. With the motor running, pour in the olive oil in a thin stream until the dressing has the consistency of single cream.

5 Season the dressing with ground black pepper and a little salt if needed. Pour it over the salad leaves and toss well, then toss in the garlic croûtons, Parmesan cheese and the remaining anchovies and serve.

WARM CHICKEN LIVER SALAD

This popular salad makes an excellent light lunch. For a more substantial dish, grill three or four rashers of streaky bacon and crumble them over the salad.

Preparation time 4–5 minutes
Cooking time 4–5 minutes

SERVES 4

*115g/4oz each fresh young spinach
leaves, rocket and lollo rosso lettuce
2 pink grapefruit
90ml/6 tbsp sunflower oil
10ml/2 tsp sesame oil
10ml/2 tsp soy sauce
225g/8oz chicken livers, chopped
salt and ground black pepper*

1 Wash, dry and tear up all the spinach and salad leaves. Mix them together well in a large salad bowl. Cut away the peel and white pith from the grapefruit, then segment them, catching the juice in a bowl. Add the segments to the leaves in the bowl.

2 Mix 60ml/4 tbsp sunflower oil with sesame oil, soy sauce and grapefruit juice to taste.

3 Heat the rest of the sunflower oil in a small pan and cook the livers for 4–5 minutes, until firm and lightly browned, stirring occasionally.

4 Tip the chicken livers over the salad. Season the dressing with salt and pepper, drizzle it over the salad and serve at once.

THAI-STYLE CABBAGE SALAD

A simple and delicious way of using cabbage. Broccoli and cauliflower can also be prepared this way.

Preparation time 6 minutes
Cooking time 4 minutes

SERVES 4–6

30ml/2 tbsp fish sauce
grated rind of 1 lime
30ml/2 tbsp lime juice
120ml/4fl oz/ ½ cup coconut milk
30ml/2 tbsp vegetable oil
2 large red chillies, seeded and finely cut into strips
6 garlic cloves, finely sliced
6 shallots, finely sliced
1 small cabbage, shredded
30ml/2 tbsp coarsely chopped roasted peanuts, to serve (optional)

1 Make the dressing. Whisk the fish sauce with the lime rind and juice and coconut milk.

2 Heat the oil in a wok or frying pan. Stir-fry the chillies, garlic and shallots, until the shallots are brown and crisp.

3 Bring a saucepan of lightly salted water to the boil. Add the cabbage and blanch for about 2 minutes. Drain thoroughly, then tip the cabbage into a bowl.

4 Stir the dressing into the cabbage, toss and mix well. Transfer the salad into a serving dish. Sprinkle with the fried shallot mixture and the coarsely chopped roasted peanuts, if using.

Curly Endive Salad with Bacon

Young dandelion leaves can replace the endive or escarole leaves and the salad is sometimes sprinkled with chopped hard-boiled egg.

Preparation time 3–4 minutes
Cooking time 6 minutes

Serves 4

225g/8oz curly endive or
    escarole leaves
75–90ml/5–6 tbsp extra virgin
    olive oil
175g/6oz piece of smoked bacon, diced,
    or 6 thick-cut smoked bacon rashers,
    cut crossways into thin strips
50g/2oz/1 cup white bread cubes
1 small garlic clove, finely chopped
15ml/1 tbsp red wine vinegar
10ml/2 tsp Dijon mustard
salt and ground black pepper

1 Tear the endive or escarole lettuce into bite-size pieces and put them in a salad bowl.

Cook's Tip
Use curly endive or escarole leaves as soon as possible after purchase. To store, wrap the leaves in a plastic bag and place in the salad drawer of the fridge for up to three days.

2 Heat 15ml/1 tbsp of the oil in a frying pan and add the bacon. Fry until crisp and browned, then remove with a slotted spoon and drain on kitchen paper.

3 Add 30ml/2 tbsp of oil to the pan and fry the bread cubes over a medium-high heat, turning frequently, until evenly browned. Remove with a slotted spoon and drain on kitchen paper.

4 Put the garlic, vinegar and mustard into the pan with the remaining oil and heat until just warm, whisking. Season to taste, then pour over the salad and sprinkle with the fried bacon and croûtons.

Green Bean and Sweet Red Pepper Salad

Preparation time 5–6 minutes
Cooking time Nil

Serves 4

350g/12oz cooked green beans,
  quartered
2 red peppers, seeded and chopped
2 spring onions, chopped
1 or more drained pickled serrano
  chillies, well rinsed and then seeded
  and chopped
1 iceberg lettuce, coarsely shredded,
  or mixed salad leaves
olives, to garnish

For the dressing
45ml/3 tbsp red wine vinegar
135ml/9 tbsp olive oil
salt and ground black pepper

1 Combine the green beans,
   peppers, spring onions and
chillies in a salad bowl.

2 Make the dressing. Pour the red
   wine vinegar into a bowl or
jug. Add salt and ground black
pepper to taste, then whisk in the
olive oil until well combined.

3 Pour half the salad dressing
   over the prepared vegetables
and toss lightly together to mix and
coat thoroughly. Taste the mixture
and add more dressing if required.
Or offer it separately.

4 Line a large platter with the
   shredded lettuce leaves and
arrange the dressed vegetable
mixture attractively on top. Garnish
with the olives and serve, with any
extra dressing.

WARM BROAD BEAN AND FETA SALAD

This recipe is loosely based on a typical medley of fresh-tasting Greek salad ingredients – broad beans, tomatoes and feta cheese. It's lovely warm or cold as a starter or main course accompaniment.

Preparation time 2 minutes
Cooking time 4–5 minutes

SERVES 4–6

900g/2lb broad beans, shelled, or
   350g/12oz frozen shelled beans
60ml/4 tbsp olive oil
175g/6oz plum tomatoes, halved, or
   quartered if large
4 garlic cloves, crushed
115g/4oz firm feta cheese, cut
   into chunks
45ml/3 tbsp chopped fresh dill, plus
   extra to garnish
12 black olives
salt and ground black pepper

1 Cook the fresh or frozen broad beans in boiling, salted water until just tender. Drain and set aside.

2 Meanwhile, heat the oil in a heavy-based frying pan and add the tomatoes and garlic. Cook over a high heat until the tomatoes are beginning to colour.

3 Add the feta to the pan and toss the ingredients together for 1 minute. Tip into a salad bowl and mix with the drained beans, dill, olives and salt and pepper. Serve garnished with chopped dill.

HALLOUMI AND GRAPE SALAD

Halloumi, a Greek cheese, is delicious fried. Its salty flavour is the ideal foil for grapes and salad greens.

Preparation time 2 minutes
Cooking time 2–3 minutes

SERVES 4

150g/5oz mixed green salad leaves
75g/3oz/ ¾ cup each seedless green
   and black grapes
250g/9oz halloumi cheese
45ml/3 tbsp olive oil
fresh young thyme leaves and basil
   sprigs, to garnish
For the dressing
60ml/4 tbsp olive oil
15ml/1 tbsp lemon juice
2.5ml/ ½ tsp caster sugar
salt and ground black pepper
15ml/1 tbsp chopped fresh thyme
   or dill

1 To make the dressing, whisk together the olive oil, lemon juice and sugar. Season with salt and pepper. Stir in the thyme or dill and set aside.

2 Toss together the salad leaves and the green and black grapes, then transfer to a large serving plate.

3 Thinly slice the cheese. Heat the oil in a large frying pan. Add the cheese and fry briefly until it turns golden on the underside. Turn the cheese with a fish slice and cook the other side.

4 Arrange the cheese over the salad. Pour over the dressing and garnish with thyme and basil.

TURKISH SALAD

This classic salad is a wonderful combination of textures and flavours. The saltiness of the cheese is perfectly balanced by the refreshing salad vegetables.

Preparation time 8–10 minutes
Cooking time Nil

SERVES 4

1 cos lettuce heart
1 green pepper
1 red pepper
½ cucumber
4 tomatoes
1 red onion
225g/8oz feta cheese, crumbled
black olives, to garnish
For the dressing
45ml/3 tbsp olive oil
45ml/3 tbsp lemon juice
1 garlic clove, crushed
15ml/1 tbsp chopped fresh parsley
15ml/1 tbsp chopped fresh mint
salt and ground black pepper

1 Chop the lettuce into bite-size pieces. Seed the peppers, remove the cores and cut the flesh into thin strips. Chop the cucumber and slice or chop the tomatoes. Cut the onion in half, then slice finely.

2 Place the chopped lettuce, peppers, cucumber, tomatoes and onion in a large bowl. Scatter the feta over the top and toss lightly.

3 Make the dressing. Whisk together the olive oil, lemon juice and garlic in a small bowl. Stir in the chopped fresh parsley and mint and season with salt and ground black pepper to taste.

4 Pour the dressing over the salad, toss lightly and serve at once, garnished with a handful of black olives.

PERSIAN SALAD

Some of the simplest dishes are also the most successful. This salad is made in minutes and has a crisp, fresh flavour. Serve it with cold meats and baked potatoes.

Preparation time 5 minutes
Cooking time Nil

SERVES 2

4 tomatoes
½ cucumber
1 onion
1 cos lettuce heart
For the dressing
30ml/2 tbsp olive oil
juice of 1 lemon
1 garlic clove, crushed
salt and ground black pepper

1 Cut the tomatoes and cucumber into small cubes. Finely chop the onion and tear the lettuce into bite-size pieces.

2 Place the tomatoes, cucumber, onion and lettuce in a large salad bowl and mix lightly together.

3 To make the dressing, pour the olive oil into a small bowl. Add the lemon juice and garlic and whisk together well. Stir in salt to taste. Pour over the salad and toss lightly to mix. Sprinkle with black pepper and serve at once.

PRAWN NOODLE SALAD WITH FRAGRANT HERBS

A light, refreshing salad with all the tangy flavour of the sea. Instead of prawns, try squid, scallops, mussels or crab.

Preparation time 8 minutes
Cooking time 1 minute

Serves 4

115g/4oz cellophane noodles, soaked
  in hot water until soft
16 cooked prawns, peeled
1 small green pepper, seeded and cut
  into strips
½ cucumber, cut into strips
1 tomato, cut into strips
2 shallots, finely sliced
salt and ground black pepper
fresh coriander leaves, to garnish
For the dressing
15ml/1 tbsp rice vinegar
30ml/2 tbsp fish sauce
30ml/2 tbsp fresh lime juice
pinch of salt
2.5ml/½ tsp grated fresh root ginger
1 lemon grass stalk, finely chopped
1 red chilli, seeded and sliced
30ml/2 tbsp roughly chopped mint
few sprigs tarragon, roughly chopped
15ml/1 tbsp snipped chives

1 Make the dressing by mixing all the ingredients in a small bowl or jug; whisk well.

2 Drain the noodles, then plunge them in a saucepan of boiling water for 1 minute. Drain, rinse under cold running water and drain again.

3 In a large bowl, combine the noodles with the prawns, pepper, cucumber, tomato and shallots. Lightly season with salt and pepper, then toss with the dressing.

4 Spoon the noodle mixture on to individual plates, arranging the prawns on top. Garnish with a few coriander leaves and serve at once.

COOK'S TIPS
Prawns are available ready-cooked and often shelled. To cook raw prawns, boil them for 5 minutes or until they turn pink. Leave them to cool in the cooking liquid, then gently pull off the tail shell and twist off the head.

THAI NOODLE SALAD

The addition of coconut milk and sesame oil gives an unusual nutty flavour to the dressing for this colourful, noodle salad.

Preparation time 5 minutes
Cooking time 5 minutes

SERVES 4–6

350g/12oz somen noodles
1 large carrot, cut into thin strips
1 bunch asparagus, trimmed and cut into 4cm/1¹/₂ in lengths
1 red pepper, seeded and cut into fine strips
115g/4oz mangetouts, topped, tailed and halved
115g/4oz baby corn cobs, halved lengthways
115g/4oz beansprouts
115g/4oz can water chestnuts, drained and finely sliced

For the dressing
45ml/3 tbsp roughly torn basil
75ml/5 tbsp roughly chopped mint
250ml/8fl oz/1 cup coconut milk
30ml/2 tbsp dark sesame oil
15ml/1 tbsp grated fresh root ginger
2 garlic cloves, finely chopped
juice of 1 lime
2 spring onions, finely chopped
salt and cayenne pepper

To garnish
1 lime, cut into wedges
50g/2oz/ ¹/₂ cup roasted peanuts, roughly chopped
fresh coriander leaves

VARIATIONS
Use shredded omelette or sliced hard-boiled eggs to garnish the salad.

1 Make the dressing. Combine the basil, mint, coconut milk, sesame oil, ginger, garlic, lime juice and spring onions in a bowl and mix well. Season to taste with salt and cayenne pepper.

2 Cook the noodles in a large saucepan of boiling water until just tender, following the directions on the packet.

3 Meanwhile, cook the vegetables in separate pans of boiling salted water until crisp-tender. Drain, plunge them into cold water and drain again. Drain and refresh the noodles in the same way.

4 Toss the noodles, vegetables and dressing together. Arrange on serving plates and garnish with the lime, peanuts and coriander.

Cabbage Slaw with Date and Apple

Three types of cabbage are shredded together for serving raw, so that the maximum amount of vitamin C is retained in this cheerful and speedy salad. It makes a very good light lunch.

Preparation time 8 minutes
Cooking time Nil

SERVES 6–8
¼ small white cabbage, shredded
¼ small red cabbage, shredded
¼ small Savoy cabbage, shredded
175g/6oz/1 cup dried stoned dates
3 eating apples
juice of 1 lemon
10ml/2 tsp caraway seeds
For the dressing
60ml/4 tbsp olive oil
15ml/1 tbsp cider vinegar
5ml/1 tsp clear honey
salt and ground black pepper

1 Finely shred all the cabbages and place the shredded cabbage in a large salad bowl.

2 Chop the dates and add them to the cabbage.

3 Core the eating apples and slice them thinly into a mixing bowl. Add the lemon juice and toss together to prevent discoloration before adding them to the salad bowl.

4 Make the dressing. Combine the oil, vinegar and honey in a screw-top jar. Add salt and pepper, then close the jar tightly and shake well. Pour the dressing over the salad, toss lightly, then sprinkle with the caraway seeds and toss again.

COOK'S TIPS
Support local orchards by looking out for different home-grown apples. Many delicious, older varieties are grown by specialist farmers, who will willingly offer a taste to would-be buyers. Choose both green and red-skinned apples if possible, to add extra colour to the salad.

Sprouted Seed Salad

If you sprout beans, lentils and whole grains, this increases their nutritional value, and they make a deliciously crunchy salad.

Preparation time 5 minutes
Cooking time Nil

SERVES 4
2 eating apples
115g/4oz/2 cups alfalfa sprouts
115g/4oz/2 cups beansprouts
115g/4oz/2 cups aduki beansprouts
¼ cucumber, sliced
1 bunch watercress, trimmed
1 carton mustard and cress, trimmed
For the dressing
150ml/¼ pint/⅔ cup low-fat natural yogurt
juice of ½ lemon
bunch of chives, snipped
30ml/2 tbsp chopped fresh herbs
ground black pepper

1 Core and slice the apples; mix with the other salad ingredients.

2 Whisk the dressing ingredients in a jug. Drizzle over the salad and toss together just before serving.

COOK'S TIP
You'll find a variety of bean and seed sprouts in the chiller cabinets of large supermarkets and health food stores. They are best used the day that you buy them, but will keep in the salad drawer of your fridge for a day or two.

CITRUS GREEN LEAF SALAD WITH CROÛTONS

Wholemeal croûtons add a delicious crunch to leaf salads. The kumquats or orange segments provide a colour contrast as well as a good helping of vitamin C.

Preparation time 4 minutes
Cooking time 1 minute

SERVES 4–6
4 kumquats or 2 seedless oranges
200g/7oz mixed green salad leaves
4 slices of wholemeal bread,
  crusts removed
30–45ml/2–3 tbsp pine nuts,
  lightly toasted
For the dressing
grated rind of 1 lemon
15ml/1 tbsp lemon juice
45ml/3 tbsp olive oil
5ml/1 tsp wholegrain mustard
1 garlic clove, crushed
salt and ground black pepper

 1 Thinly slice the kumquats, or peel and segment the oranges.

COOK'S TIP
Kumquats look like tiny oval oranges. The skin is edible.

2 Tear all the salad leaves into bite-size pieces and mix together in a large salad bowl.

3 Toast the bread on both sides and cut into cubes. Add to the salad leaves with the sliced kumquats or orange segments.

4 Shake all the dressing ingredients together in a jar. Pour over the salad just before serving and scatter the toasted pine nuts over the top.

MIXED BEAN SALAD WITH TOMATO DRESSING

All pulses are a good source of vegetable protein, and minerals; this hearty salad makes a meal.

Preparation time 3–4 minutes
Cooking time 5–6 minutes

SERVES 4
115g/4oz French beans
425g/15oz can mixed pulses, drained,
  rinsed and drained again
2 celery sticks, finely chopped
1 small onion, finely chopped
3 tomatoes, chopped
chopped fresh parsley, to garnish
For the dressing
45ml/3 tbsp olive oil
10ml/2 tsp red wine vinegar
1 garlic clove, crushed
15ml/1 tbsp tomato chutney
salt and ground black pepper

1 Remove the ends from the French beans, then cook them in boiling water for 5–6 minutes until tender. Drain, refresh under cold running water, drain again and cut into thirds.

2 Place the beans and pulses in a large bowl. Add the celery, onion and tomatoes and toss to mix.

3 Shake the dressing ingredients together in a jar. Pour over the salad and sprinkle with the parsley.

COOK'S TIP
Cans of mixed pulses include several different types, such as chick-peas, pinto, black-eye, red kidney, soya and aduki beans, and save the hassle of long soaking and cooking that dried beans require.

SPINACH WITH RAISINS AND PINE NUTS

Raisins and pine nuts are frequent partners in Spanish recipes. Here, tossed with wilted spinach and croûtons, they make a delicious and swiftly prepared snack.

Preparation time 2 minutes
Cooking time 5 minutes

SERVES 4
50g/2oz/ ⅓ cup raisins
1 thick slice crusty white bread
45ml/3 tbsp olive oil
25g/1oz/ ⅓ cup pine nuts
500g/1¼lb young spinach leaves,
  stalks removed
2 garlic cloves, crushed
salt and ground black pepper

1   Put the raisins in a small bowl. Pour over boiling water to cover and leave to soak while you make the croûtons and prepare the rest of the salad ingredients.

2   Cut the bread into cubes and discard the crusts. Heat 30ml/ 2 tbsp of the oil and fry the bread until golden. Drain.

3   Heat the remaining oil in the pan. Fry the pine nuts until beginning to colour. Add the spinach and garlic and cook quickly, turning the spinach until it has just wilted.

4   Drain the raisins and add them to the pan. Toss gently and season lightly with salt and pepper. Transfer to a warmed serving dish. Scatter with the croûtons and serve the salad at once.

VARIATIONS
When you have a little more time, use Swiss chard or spinach beet instead of the spinach. They need to be cooked for slightly longer, but both have very good flavour.

BALTI MUSHROOMS IN A CREAMY GARLIC SAUCE

This is a simple and delicious recipe, which could be served on Granary toast or with basmati rice.

Preparation time 5 minutes
Cooking time 5 minutes

SERVES 4

350g/12oz/3 cups button mushrooms
45ml/3 tbsp olive oil
1 bay leaf
3 garlic cloves, roughly chopped
2 green chillies, seeded and chopped
225g/8oz/1 cup fromage frais
15ml/1 tbsp chopped fresh mint
15ml/1 tbsp chopped fresh coriander
5ml/1 tsp salt
fresh mint and coriander leaves,
  to garnish

1. Unless they are very small, cut the mushrooms in half. Set them aside in a bowl.

2. Heat the oil in a non-stick wok or balti pan, then add the bay leaf, garlic and chillies and cook for about 1 minute.

3. Add the mushrooms. Stir-fry for about 2 minutes.

COOK'S TIP
Cook the mushrooms for longer if you like them well cooked and browned.

4. Remove from the heat and stir in the fromage frais followed by the mint, coriander and salt. Heat, stirring for 2 minutes, then transfer to a warmed serving dish, garnish with the mint and coriander leaves and serve at once.

VEGETABLE AND EGG NOODLE RIBBONS

Serve this elegant, colourful dish with a tossed green salad as a light lunch. Use fresh pasta for optimum speed and flavour.

Preparation time 3 minutes
Cooking time 7 minutes

SERVES 4
1 large carrot, peeled
2 courgettes
50g/2oz/¼ cup butter
15ml/1 tbsp olive oil
6 fresh shiitake mushrooms,
  finely sliced
50g/2oz/½ cup frozen peas, thawed
350g/12oz broad egg ribbon noodles
10ml/2 tsp chopped fresh mixed
  herbs, such as marjoram, chives
  and basil
salt and ground black pepper
25g/1oz Parmesan cheese, to
  serve (optional)

1 Using a vegetable peeler, carefully slice thin strips from the carrot and from the courgettes.

2 Heat the butter with the olive oil in a large frying pan. Stir in the carrots and shiitake mushrooms; fry for 2 minutes. Add the courgettes and peas and stir-fry until the courgettes are cooked, but still crisp. Season with salt and pepper.

3 Meanwhile, cook the noodles in a large saucepan of boiling water until just tender. Drain the noodles well and tip them into a bowl. Add the vegetables and toss gently to mix.

4 Sprinkle over the fresh herbs and season to taste. If using the Parmesan cheese, grate or shave it over the top. Toss lightly and serve.

BUCKWHEAT NOODLES WITH GOAT'S CHEESE

When you don't feel like doing a lot of cooking, try this good, fast supper dish. The earthy flavour of buckwheat goes well with the nutty, peppery taste of rocket leaves, and both are offset by the deliciously creamy goat's cheese.

Preparation and
cooking time 8–10 minutes

SERVES 4
350g/12oz buckwheat noodles
50g/2oz/¼ cup butter
2 garlic cloves, finely chopped
4 shallots, sliced
75g/3oz/¾ cup hazelnuts, lightly
  roasted and roughly chopped
large handful rocket leaves
175g/6oz goat's cheese
salt and ground black pepper

1 Bring a large saucepan of lightly salted water to a rolling boil and add the noodles. Cook until just tender.

2 Meanwhile, heat the butter in a large frying pan. Add the garlic and shallots and cook for 2–3 minutes, stirring all the time, until the shallots are soft. Do not let the garlic brown.

3 Drain the noodles well. Add the hazelnuts to the pan and fry for about 1 minute. Add the rocket leaves and, when they start to wilt, toss in the noodles and heat through.

4 Season with salt and pepper. Crumble in the goat's cheese and serve immediately.

MELON AND STRAWBERRY SALAD

A beautiful and colourful fruit salad, this is a particularly good dessert to serve after a spicy main course. For speed, cube the melons.

Preparation time 8–10 minutes
Cooking time Nil

SERVES 4
1 galia melon
1 honeydew melon
¹/₂ watermelon
225g/8oz/2 cups fresh strawberries
15ml/1 tbsp lemon juice
15ml/1 tbsp clear honey
15ml/1 tbsp water
15ml/1 tbsp chopped fresh mint
1 mint sprig, to garnish (optional)

1 Prepare the melons by cutting them in half and discarding the seeds. Use a melon baller to scoop out the flesh into balls, or cut it into cubes with a knife. Place the melon balls (or cubes) in a fruit bowl.

2 Rinse and take the stems off the strawberries, cut these in half and add them to the fruit bowl.

3 Mix together the lemon juice, clear honey and water. Stir carefully to blend and then pour over the fruit. Stir the fruit so that it is thoroughly coated in the lemon and honey mixture.

4 Sprinkle the chopped mint over the top of the fruit. Serve garnished with the mint sprig, if you like.

COOK'S TIP
Use whichever melons are available: substitute cantaloupe for galia or charentais for watermelon, for example. However, try to find three different kinds of melon so that you get variation in colour, and also a variety of textures and flavours.

FIGS WITH RICOTTA CREAM

*Fresh, ripe figs are full of natural
sweetness, and need little adornment.
This simple recipe makes the most of
their beautiful, intense flavour.*

Preparation time 3–4 minutes
Cooking time Nil

SERVES 4

*4 ripe, fresh figs
115g/4oz/ ½ cup ricotta or
    cottage cheese
45ml/3 tbsp crème fraîche
15ml/1 tbsp clear honey
2.5ml/ ½ tsp pure vanilla essence
freshly grated nutmeg, to decorate*

1 Trim the stalks from the figs.
   Make four cuts through each fig
from the stalk-end, cutting them
almost through but leaving them
joined at the base.

3 Mix together the ricotta or
   cottage cheese, crème fraîche,
honey and vanilla essence.

VARIATION
Use full-fat soft cheese instead of ricotta
or cottage cheese and Greek yogurt in
place of the crème fraîche.

4 Spoon a little ricotta cream on
   to each plate and sprinkle with
grated nutmeg to serve.

2 Place the figs on serving plates
   and ease the cuts apart gently
to open them out.

EMERALD FRUIT SALAD

The cool, green-coloured fruits make a refreshing — and fast — dessert.

Preparation and cooking time 8 minutes

SERVES 4

30ml/2 tbsp lime juice
30ml/2 tbsp clear honey
2 green eating apples, cored and sliced
1 small ripe melon, diced
2 kiwi fruit, sliced
1 star fruit, sliced
fresh mint sprigs, to decorate
yogurt or fromage frais, to serve

1 Mix together the lime juice and honey in a large bowl, then toss the apple slices in this.

2 Stir in the melon, kiwi fruit and star fruit. Place in a glass serving dish.

3 Decorate the fruit salad with mint sprigs and serve with yogurt or fromage frais.

VARIATIONS

Add other green fruits when available, such as greengages, grapes, pears or kiwano, which is a type of melon. It has a tough yellowy orange rind covered with sharp spikes, and the flesh inside looks like a bright green jelly, encasing edible seeds, which can be removed with a spoon. If time permits, chill the salad for an hour or two before serving. It is delicious with extra-thick cream to which a couple of spoonfuls of advocaat or eggnog have been added.

Warm Bagels with Poached Apricots

Preparation time 2 minutes
Cooking time 8 minutes

SERVES 4

a few strips of orange peel
225g/8oz/1¹/₃ cups ready-to-eat
  dried apricots
250ml/8fl oz/1 cup orange juice
2.5ml/¹/₂ tsp orange flower water
2 cinnamon and raisin bagels
20ml/4 tsp orange marmalade
60ml/4 tbsp crème fraîche or
  soured cream
15g/¹/₂oz/2 tbsp chopped pistachio
  nuts, to decorate

1 Cut the strips of orange peel into fine shreds. Cook them in boiling water until softened, then drain and place in cold water.

2 Preheat the oven to 160°C/ 325°F/Gas 3. Combine the apricots and orange juice in a small saucepan. Simmer for about 6 minutes until the juice has reduced and looks syrupy. Allow to cool, then stir in the orange flower water. Meanwhile, place the bagels on a baking sheet and warm in the oven for 5–10 minutes.

3 Split the bagels in half horizontally. Lay one half, crumb uppermost, on each serving plate. Spread 5ml/1 tsp orange marmalade on each bagel.

4 Spoon 15ml/1 tbsp crème fraîche or soured cream into the centre of each bagel and place a quarter of the apricot compôte at the side. Scatter orange peel and pistachio nuts over the top to decorate. Serve immediately.

Cook's Tip
When you remove the strips of rind from the orange, use a swivel-action vegetable peeler to obtain thin strips and avoid removing any of the bitter white pith with the rind.

BRAZILIAN COFFEE BANANAS

Rich, lavish and sinful-looking, this is one of the fastest desserts: a must in the quick cook's repertoire.

Preparation time 4 minutes
Cooking time Nil

SERVES 4

4 small ripe bananas
15ml/1 tbsp instant coffee granules
15ml/1 tbsp hot water
30ml/2 tbsp dark muscovado sugar
250g/9oz/generous 1 cup Greek yogurt
15ml/1 tbsp toasted flaked almonds

1 Peel and slice one banana and mash the remaining three with a fork. Set the sliced banana aside.

2 Dissolve the coffee granules in the hot water and stir into the mashed bananas.

3 Spoon a little of the mashed banana mixture into four serving dishes and sprinkle with the muscovado sugar. Top with a spoonful of yogurt, then repeat until all the ingredients are used up.

4 Swirl the last layer of yogurt for a marbled effect. Finish with a few banana slices and the flaked almonds. Serve immediately, or the bananas will discolour.

HOT BANANAS WITH RUM AND RAISINS

Choose almost-ripe bananas with evenly coloured skins, either all yellow or just green at the tips.

Preparation time 2 minutes
Cooking time 3–4 minutes

SERVES 4

40g/1½oz/¼ cup seedless raisins
75ml/5 tbsp dark rum
50g/2oz/¼ cup unsalted butter
60ml/4 tbsp soft light brown sugar
4 ripe bananas, peeled and halved
   lengthways
1.5ml/¼ tsp grated nutmeg
1.5ml/¼ tsp ground cinnamon
30ml/2 tbsp slivered almonds, toasted
chilled cream or vanilla ice cream,
   to serve (optional)

1   Put the raisins in a bowl with the rum. Leave them to soak while you fry the bananas.

2   Melt the butter in a frying pan, add the sugar and stir until dissolved. Add the bananas and cook for a few minutes until tender.

3   Sprinkle the spices over the bananas, then pour over the rum and raisins. Carefully set alight using a long taper and stir gently.

4   Scatter over the slivered almonds and serve immediately with chilled cream or ice cream.

ETON MESS

This dish is enjoyed by parents and pupils picnicking on the lawns at Eton College's annual prize-giving in June. Chill the strawberries in Kirsch if you have time.

Preparation time 7 minutes
Cooking time Nil

Serves 4
500g/1¼lb/5 cups strawberries, chopped
45–60ml/3–4 tbsp Kirsch
300ml/½ pint/1¼ cups double cream
6 small white meringues
fresh mint sprigs, to decorate

1 Put the strawberries in a bowl, sprinkle over the Kirsch, then set aside for 3–4 minutes.

2 Whip the cream until soft peaks form, then gently fold in the strawberries with their juices.

3 Crush the meringues into rough chunks, then scatter over the strawberry mixture and fold in gently.

4 Spoon the strawberry mixture into a glass serving bowl, decorate with mint sprigs and serve immediately.

COOK'S TIP
If you would prefer to make a less rich version, use strained Greek yogurt or thick natural yogurt instead of part or all of the cream. Simply beat the yogurt gently before adding the strawberry and Kirsch mixture.

ICE CREAM STRAWBERRY SHORTCAKE

This pudding is an American classic, and couldn't be easier to make. Fresh juicy strawberries, store-bought flan cases and rich ice cream are all you need to create a creamy dessert.

Preparation time 10 minutes
Cooking time Nil

SERVES 4

*3 x 15cm/6in ready-made sponge
  flan cases or shortbreads
675g/1¹/₂lb/6 cups strawberries
1.2 litres/2 pints/5 cups vanilla or
  strawberry ice cream
icing sugar, for dusting*

1 If using sponge flan cases, trim the raised edges with a serrated knife.

2 Hull and halve the strawberries. Spoon one-third of the ice cream on to a flan case or shortbread layer, placing it in scoops, with one-third of the strawberries in between.

3 Spoon more strawberries and ice cream on to a second flan or shortbread layer and place it on top of the first, then add the final layer, piling the strawberries up high.

COOK'S TIPS
Don't worry if the shortcake falls apart a little when you cut into it. It may look messy, but it will taste marvellous. If time permits, the dessert can be assembled up to an hour before serving and kept in the freezer without spoiling the fruit.

Mandarins in Orange Flower Syrup

You can cheat with this recipe, and buy canned whole peeled mandarins or clementines. Use fresh orange juice for the syrup. You can serve the dessert as soon as you make it, but it is even better chilled.

Preparation time 10 minutes
Cooking time Nil

Serves 4

10 mandarins
15ml/1 tbsp icing sugar
10ml/2 tsp orange flower water
15ml/1 tbsp chopped pistachio nuts

1 Thinly pare a little of the coloured zest from one mandarin and cut it into fine shreds for decoration. Squeeze the juice from two mandarins and reserve it.

2 Peel the remaining fruit, removing as much of the white pith as possible. Arrange the whole fruit in a wide dish.

3 Mix the reserved juice, icing sugar and orange flower water and pour it over the fruit. Cover the dish and chill for 5 minutes.

4 Meanwhile, blanch the shreds of zest in boiling water for 30 seconds. Drain and leave to cool. Sprinkle them over the mandarins, with the pistachio nuts, to serve.

PAPAYA SKEWERS WITH PASSION FRUIT COULIS

Fresh-tasting tropical fruits, full of natural sweetness, make a simple, exotic dessert.

Preparation time 7–8 minutes
Cooking time Nil

SERVES 6

3 ripe papayas
10 passion fruit or kiwi fruit
30ml/2 tbsp lime juice
30ml/2 tbsp icing sugar
30ml/2 tbsp white rum
lime slices, to decorate

1 Cut the papayas in half and scoop out the seeds. Peel them and cut the flesh into even-size chunks. Thread the chunks on to six bamboo skewers.

2 Cut eight of the passion fruit in half and scoop out the flesh with a teaspoon. Purée the flesh for a few seconds in a blender or food processor. If using kiwi fruit, slice off the top and bottom from eight of the fruits, then remove the skin. Cut the kiwi fruit in half and purée them briefly.

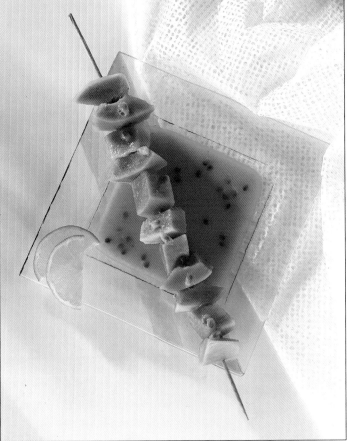

3 Press the pulp through a sieve placed over a bowl and discard the seeds. Add the lime juice, icing sugar and rum, and stir until the sugar has dissolved.

4 Spoon a little coulis on to six serving plates. Arrange the skewers on top. Scoop the flesh from the remaining passion fruit and spoon it over or slice the kiwi fruit and add it. Decorate with the lime slices.

COOK'S TIP

If you are short of time, the passion fruit flesh can be used as it is, without puréeing or sieving. Simply scoop the flesh from the skins and mix it with the lime, sugar and rum. Kiwi fruit will still need to be puréed, however.

QUICK APRICOT BLENDER WHIP

This is one of the quickest desserts you could make — and also one of the prettiest.

Preparation time 4 minutes
Cooking time 2 minutes

SERVES 4

400g/14oz can apricot halves in juice
15ml/1 tbsp Grand Marnier
  or brandy
175ml/6fl oz/ ¾ cup Greek yogurt
30ml/2 tbsp flaked almonds

COOK'S TIP

For an even lighter dessert, use low-fat instead of Greek yogurt, and, if you prefer to omit the liqueur, add a little of the fruit juice from the can.

1 Drain the juice from the apricots and place the fruit and in a blender or food processor with the liqueur.

2 Process the apricots until they are smooth.

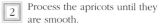

3 Spoon the fruit purée and yogurt in alternate spoonfuls into four tall glasses or glass dishes, swirling them together slightly to give a marbled effect.

4 Lightly toast the almonds until they are golden. Let them cool slightly and then sprinkle some on top of each dessert.

RASPBERRY AND PASSION FRUIT SWIRLS

If passion fruit is not available, just use extra raspberries.

Preparation time 4–5 minutes
Cooking time Nil

SERVES 4

300g/11oz/2 cups raspberries
2 passion fruit
400g/14oz/1¾ cups low-fat
fromage frais
30ml/2 tbsp caster sugar
raspberries and sprigs of mint,
to decorate

1 Mash the raspberries in a small bowl with a fork until the juice runs. Scoop out the passion fruit pulp into a separate bowl, and mix in the fromage frais and sugar.

3 Decorate each dessert with a whole raspberry and a sprig of fresh mint. Serve at once.

2 Spoon alternate spoonfuls of the raspberry pulp and the fromage frais mixture into stemmed glasses or one large serving dish, stirring lightly to create a gentle swirled effect.

ITALIAN RICOTTA PUDDING
🌾 🌾

This creamy, rich dessert is very easy to make. Ideally, it should be chilled before serving (and can be made up to 24 hours ahead) but it can be served within minutes of making. Just pop it in the freezer while you eat your main course.

**Preparation time 5–6 minutes
Cooking time Nil**

SERVES 4–6
*225g/8oz/1 cup ricotta cheese
50g/2oz/ ¹/₃ cup candied fruits
60ml/4 tbsp sweet Marsala
250ml/8fl oz/1 cup double cream
50g/2oz/ ¹/₄ cup caster sugar, plus
  extra to serve
finely grated rind of 1 orange
350g/12oz/2 cups fresh raspberries
strips of thinly pared orange rind,
  to decorate*

1 Press the ricotta through a sieve into a bowl. Finely chop the candied fruits and stir into the sieved ricotta with half the Marsala. Put the cream, sugar and orange rind in another bowl and whip until the cream is standing in soft peaks.

2 Fold the whipped cream into the ricotta mixture. Spoon into individual glass serving bowls and top with the raspberries.

3 Sprinkle the raspberries with the remaining Marsala and dust the top of each dessert liberally with caster sugar. Decorate with the strips of pared orange rind and serve.

> COOK'S TIP
> Buy candied fruits in large pieces from a good delicatessen – tubs of chopped candied peel are too tough to eat raw, and should only be used in baking.

CHOCOLATE FUDGE SUNDAES

Preparation time 3 minutes
Cooking time 6 minutes

SERVES 4

4 scoops each vanilla and coffee
  ice cream
2 small ripe bananas, sliced
whipped cream
toasted flaked almonds
For the sauce
50g/2oz/ ¹/₃ cup soft light brown sugar
120ml/4fl oz/ ¹/₂ cup golden syrup
45ml/3 tbsp strong black coffee
5ml/1 tsp ground cinnamon
150g/5oz plain chocolate, chopped
75ml/3fl oz/ ¹/₃ cup whipping cream
45ml/3 tbsp coffee liqueur (optional)

1. To make the sauce, place the sugar, syrup, coffee and cinnamon in a heavy-based saucepan. Bring to the boil, then boil for about 5 minutes, stirring.

2. Turn off the heat, leave to cool for 1 minute, then and stir in the chopped chocolate. When melted and smooth, stir in the cream and liqueur, if using. Leave to cool a little while you assemble the sundaes.

3. Fill four tall glasses with a small scoop each of vanilla and coffee ice cream.

4. Scatter the sliced bananas over the ice cream. Pour the warm fudge sauce over the bananas, then top each sundae with a generous swirl of whipped cream. Sprinkle with toasted flaked almonds and serve at once.

VARIATIONS

Ring the changes by choosing other flavours of ice cream. Strawberry, toffee or chocolate work well. In the summer, substitute raspberries or strawberries for the bananas, and scatter chopped roasted hazelnuts on top in place of the flaked almonds.

20 MINUTE RECIPES

It may surprise you to find just how many delicious dishes can be prepared in twenty minutes. In less time than it takes to reheat a frozen meal, you can impress your guests with Poached Eggs with Spinach or Pan-steamed Mussels with Thai Herbs. Pasta really is faster these days, with fresh and quick-cook varieties readily available, so celebrate with Tagliatelle with Tomatoes and Black Olives. For a final flourish, try Apple Soufflé Omelette or Orange Yogurt Brûlées.

Fresh Tomato Soup with Cheese Croûtes

Intensely flavoured sun-ripened tomatoes need little embellishment in this fresh-tasting soup. If you buy from the supermarket, choose the ripest-looking ones and adjust the amount of sugar and vinegar, depending on the tomatoes' natural sweetness. On a hot day, this Italian soup is also delicious chilled.

Preparation time 5 minutes
Cooking time 13–14 minutes

SERVES 6

1.5kg/3–3 ½ lb ripe tomatoes
400ml/14fl oz/1 ⅔ cups chicken or
   vegetable stock
45ml/3 tbsp sun-dried tomato paste
30–45ml/2–3 tbsp balsamic vinegar
10–15ml/2–3 tsp caster sugar
small handful fresh basil leaves, plus
   a few extra to garnish
salt and ground black pepper
toasted cheese croûtes and crème
   fraîche, to serve

1 Mark the tomatoes with a small cross at the base, plunge them into boiling water for 30 seconds, then refresh in cold water. Peel away the skins and quarter the tomatoes. Put them in a large saucepan and pour over the chicken or vegetable stock. Bring just to the boil, reduce the heat, cover and simmer gently for about 10 minutes or until all the tomatoes are pulpy.

2 Stir in the tomato paste, vinegar, sugar and basil. Season with salt and pepper, then cook gently, stirring, for 2 minutes.

3 Process the soup in a blender or food processor, then return to the pan and reheat gently.

4 Serve in heated bowls. Top each portion with one or two toasted cheese croûtes and a spoonful of crème fraîche, garnished with the basil leaves.

COOK'S TIPS
Use good-quality stock for this soup. If you don't have time to make your own stock – or feel that life's too short for such worthy pursuits – buy superior stock in a can or carton.

RED PEPPER SOUP WITH CHILLI AND LIME

The beautiful rich red colour of this soup makes it a very attractive starter or light lunch.

Preparation and cooking time 20 minutes

SERVES 4–6

4 red peppers, seeded and chopped
1 large onion, chopped
5ml/1 tsp olive oil
1 garlic clove, crushed
1 small red chilli, seeded and sliced
45ml/3 tbsp tomato purée
900ml/1 ½ pints/3 ¾ cups chicken
   stock
finely grated rind and juice
   of 1 lime
salt and ground black pepper
shreds of pared lime rind, to garnish

1 Cook the peppers and onion gently in the oil in a covered saucepan for about 5 minutes, shaking the pan occasionally.

2 Stir in the garlic, then add the chilli with the tomato purée. Stir in half the stock, then bring to the boil. Cover the pan, lower the heat and simmer for 10 minutes.

3 Purée the mixture in a food processor or blender. Return to the pan, then add the rest of the stock.

4 Add the grated lime rind and juice to the soup, with salt and pepper to taste. Bring the soup back to the boil, then serve at once with strips of lime rind scattered into each bowl.

COOK'S TIPS
Yellow or orange peppers could be substituted for the red peppers. If you haven't got a fresh chilli (or don't have time to seed and slice one), add a dash or two of Tabasco sauce to the soup instead.

SPANISH GARLIC SOUP

This is a simple and satisfying soup, made with one of the most popular ingredients in the quick cook's kitchen — garlic!

Preparation time 2 minutes
Cooking time 12 minutes

SERVES 4
30ml/2 tbsp olive oil
4 large garlic cloves, peeled
4 slices French bread, about 5 mm/
  ¼ in thick
15ml/1 tbsp paprika
1 litre/1 ¾ pints/4 cups beef stock
1.5ml/ ¼ tsp ground cumin
pinch of saffron strands
4 eggs
salt and ground black pepper
chopped fresh parsley, to garnish

1 Preheat the oven to 230°C/
450°F/Gas 8. Heat the oil in a large pan. Add the whole garlic cloves and cook until golden. Remove and set aside. Fry the bread in the oil until golden, then set aside.

2 Add the paprika to the pan, and fry for a few seconds. Stir in the beef stock, cumin and saffron, then add the reserved garlic, crushing the cloves with the back of a wooden spoon. Season with salt and pepper then cook for about 5 minutes.

3 Ladle the soup into four ovenproof bowls and break an egg into each. Place a slice of fried bread on top of each egg, then put the bowls in the oven for about 3–4 minutes, until the eggs are set. Sprinkle each portion with parsley and serve at once.

COOK'S TIP
When you switch the oven on, put a baking sheet in at the same time. Stand the soup bowls on the hot baking sheet when you put them in the oven and you will be able to remove them quickly and easily as soon as the eggs have set.

FRESH PEA SOUP

You really need fresh peas for this soup, but podding them can be time-consuming. Delegate the job to young kitchen hands if you can, or use frozen peas, thawing and rinsing them before use.

Preparation time 2–5 minutes
Cooking time 15 minutes

SERVES 2–3

small knob of butter
2 or 3 shallots, finely chopped
400g/14oz/3 cups shelled fresh peas
   (from about 1.4kg/3lb garden peas)
   or thawed frozen peas
475ml/16fl oz/2 cups water
45–60ml/3–4 tbsp whipping cream
   (optional)
salt and ground black pepper
croûtons or crumbled crisp bacon,
   to garnish

[1] Melt the butter in a heavy saucepan or flameproof casserole. Add the shallots and cook for about 3 minutes, stirring occasionally.

COOK'S TIP
If you use frozen peas for the soup, cook them in flavoursome vegetable stock or light chicken stock instead of water, as they will lack the delicate flavour of freshly podded garden peas. Instead of stirring the cream into the soup, swirl it on top when serving.

[2] Add the peas and water and season with salt and a little pepper. Cover and simmer for about 12 minutes for young or frozen peas and up to 15 minutes for large or older peas, stirring occasionally.

[3] When the peas are tender, ladle them into a food processor or blender with a little of the cooking liquid and process until smooth.

[4] Strain the pea soup into the saucepan or casserole, stir in the cream, if using, and heat through without boiling. Add seasoning and serve hot, garnished with croûtons or bacon.

HADDOCK AND BROCCOLI CHOWDER

A warming main-meal soup for hearty appetites.

Preparation time 5 minutes
Cooking time 15 minutes

SERVES 4

4 spring onions, sliced
450g/1lb new potatoes, diced
300ml/ ½ pint/1¼ cups water
300ml// ½ pint/1¼ cups milk
1 bay leaf
225g/8oz/2 cups broccoli
* florets, sliced*
450g/1lb smoked haddock
* fillets, skinned*
200g/7oz can sweetcorn, drained
ground black pepper
chopped spring onions, to garnish

1 Place the spring onions and potatoes in a large saucepan and add the water, milk and bay leaf. Bring the liquid to the boil, then cover the pan, lower the heat and simmer for 8 minutes.

2 Add the broccoli. Cut the fish into bite-size chunks and add to the pan with the sweetcorn.

3 Season the mixture well with black pepper, then cover the pan and simmer for 5 minutes more, or until the fish is cooked through. Remove the bay leaf and scatter over the spring onions. Serve the soup hot, with crusty bread.

COOK'S TIPS

New potatoes are now available for most of the year. To save time, buy packs of ready-prepared new or salad potatoes, so all you have to do is dice them.

VARIATIONS

Smoked cod fillets would be equally good in this chowder, or, if you prefer, substitute white cod or haddock fillets for half or all of the smoked fish.

CORN AND CRAB CHOWDER

Chowder comes from the French word meaning a large cooking pot. This is what the fishermen on the east coast of North America used for boiling up whatever was left over from the sale of their catch for supper.

Preparation time 5 minutes
Cooking time 14 minutes

SERVES 4

25g/1oz/2 tbsp butter
1 small onion, chopped
350g/12oz can sweetcorn, drained
600ml/1 pint/2½ cups milk
175g/6oz can white crabmeat,
    drained and flaked
115g/4oz/1 cup peeled,
    cooked prawns
2 spring onions, finely chopped
150ml/¼ pint/⅔ cup single cream or
    creamy milk
pinch of cayenne pepper
salt and ground black pepper
4 cooked prawns in shells, to garnish

1. Melt the butter in a large saucepan and gently fry the onion for 4–5 minutes, until softened.

2. Reserve 30ml/2 tbsp of the sweetcorn for the garnish and add the remainder to the pan with the milk. Bring the milk to the boil, then lower the heat, cover the pan and simmer stirring occasionally, for 5 minutes.

3. Pour the sweetcorn mixture, in batches if necessary, into a blender or food processor and whizz until smooth.

4. Return the mixture to the pan and stir in the crabmeat, prawns, spring onions, cream or milk and cayenne pepper. Reheat gently.

5. Meanwhile, place the reserved sweetcorn kernels in a small frying pan without oil and dry-fry over a medium heat until golden and toasted. Season the soup well and serve each bowlful topped with a few of the toasted kernels and a whole prawn.

CHILLI BEEF NACHOS

The addition of minced beef to this traditional starter demonstrates the use of mince as an excellent extender, creating a filling, quick meal.

Preparation time 3–4 minutes
Cooking time 14–15 minutes

SERVES 4
225g/8oz/1 cup minced beef
2 red chillies, chopped
3 spring onions, chopped
175g/6oz nachos
300ml/ ½ pint/1 ¼ cups soured cream
50g/2oz/ ½ cup freshly grated
    Cheddar cheese
salt and ground black pepper

1 Dry-fry the minced beef and chillies in a large pan for about 10 minutes, stirring all the time.

2 Add the spring onions, season well and cook for a further 2 minutes. Preheat the grill.

3 Arrange the nachos in four individual flameproof dishes.

4 Spoon on the minced beef mixture, top with dollops of soured cream and sprinkle with the grated cheese. Grill under a medium heat for 2–3 minutes or until the cheese is bubbling. Serve at once.

BREADED SOLE BATONS

Crisp, crumbed fish strips — almost as speedy but smarter than fish fingers.

Preparation time 10–12 minutes
Cooking time 6–7 minutes

SERVES 4

275g/10oz lemon sole fillets, skinned
2 eggs
115g/4oz/2 cups fine fresh
 breadcrumbs
75g/3oz/ ³/₄ cup plain flour
salt and ground black pepper
oil, for frying
lemon wedges and tartare sauce,
 to serve

1 Cut the fish fillets into long diagonal strips each measuring about 2cm/³/₄ in wide.

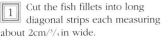

2 Break the eggs into a shallow dish and beat well with a fork. Place the breadcrumbs in another shallow dish. Put the flour in a large polythene bag and season with salt and ground black pepper.

3 Dip the fish strips in the egg, turning to coat well. Place on a plate and then shake a few at a time in the bag of seasoned flour. Dip the fish strips in the egg again and then in the breadcrumbs, turning to coat well. Place on a tray in a single layer, not touching. Let the coating set for at least 5 minutes.

4 Heat 1cm/¹/₂ in oil in a large frying pan over a medium-high heat. When the oil is hot (a cube of bread will sizzle) fry the fish strips in batches for about 2–2¹/₂ minutes, turning once, taking care not to overcrowd the pan. Drain on kitchen paper and keep warm. Serve the fish with tartare sauce and lemon wedges.

SMOKED MACKEREL AND APPLE DIP

This quick, fishy dip is served with tasty, curried dippers.

Preparation time 5 minutes
Cooking time 10 minutes

SERVES 6–8

350g/12oz smoked mackerel, skinned and boned
1 soft eating apple, peeled, cored and cut into chunks
150ml/ ¼ pint/ ⅔ cup fromage frais
pinch paprika or curry powder
salt and ground black pepper
apple slices, to garnish
For the dippers
25g/1oz/2 tbsp butter, softened
5ml/1 tsp curry paste
4 slices white bread, crusts removed

1 Place the smoked mackerel in a food processor with the apple, fromage frais and seasonings.

2 Blend for about 2 minutes or until the mixture is really smooth. Check the seasoning, then transfer to a small serving dish.

3 Preheat the oven to 200°C/ 400°F/Gas 6. To make the dippers, place the bread on a baking sheet. Blend the butter and curry paste; then spread over the bread.

4 Cook the bread in the oven for about 10 minutes, or until crisp and golden. Cut into fingers and serve immediately, with the mackerel dip, garnished with the apple slices.

COOK'S TIP
Instead of using plain sliced bread, try other breads for the dippers – Italian ciabatta, wholemeal, rye, or pitta breads would be excellent.

BAKED EGGS WITH TARRAGON

Traditional cocotte dishes or small ramekins are ideal for this recipe.

Preparation time 1 minute
Cooking time 10–11 minutes

SERVES 4

40g/1½oz/3 tbsp butter
120ml/4fl oz/½ cup double cream
15–30ml/1–2 tbsp chopped fresh tarragon
4 eggs
salt and ground black pepper
fresh tarragon sprigs, to garnish

1 Preheat the oven to 180°C/ 350°F/Gas 4. Lightly butter four small ovenproof dishes, then warm them in the oven briefly.

2 Gently warm the cream. Sprinkle some tarragon into each dish, then spoon in some cream.

3 Carefully break an egg into each of the prepared ovenproof dishes, season the eggs with salt and pepper and spoon a little more of the cream over each of the eggs.

4 Add a small knob of butter to each dish and place them in a roasting tin. Pour in hot water to come halfway up the sides of the dishes. Bake for 8–10 minutes, until the whites are just set and the yolks still soft. Garnish with tarragon.

POACHED EGGS WITH SPINACH

This classic recipe dish can be served as a starter, but is also excellent for a light lunch or brunch.

Preparation time 2 minutes
Cooking time 12 minutes

SERVES 4

25g/1oz/2 tbsp butter
450g/1lb young spinach leaves
2.5ml/ ½ tsp vinegar
4 eggs
salt and ground black pepper
For the hollandaise sauce
175g/6oz/ ¾ cup butter, cut into
  small pieces
2 egg yolks
15ml/1 tbsp lemon juice
15ml/1 tbsp water
salt and ground white pepper

COOK'S TIP
Hollandaise sauce is quick and easy to make in a blender or food processor. If you wish, you can make it an hour or two in advance and keep it warm in a wide-mouthed vacuum flask.

1 To make the hollandaise sauce, melt the butter in a small saucepan over a medium heat until it bubbles, then remove from the heat.

2 Put the egg yolks, lemon juice and water into a blender or food processor and whizz to blend. With the machine running, slowly pour in the hot butter in a thin stream. Stop pouring when you reach the milky solids at the bottom of the pan. When the sauce thickens, season and add more lemon juice if needed. Transfer the sauce to a bowl, cover and keep warm.

3 Melt the butter in a heavy frying pan over a medium heat. Add the spinach and cook until wilted, stirring occasionally. Season and keep warm.

4 To poach the eggs, bring a medium pan of lightly salted water to the boil and add the vinegar. Break an egg into a saucer and slide the egg into the water. Reduce the heat and simmer for a few minutes until the white is set and the yolk is still soft. Remove with a slotted spoon and drain. Trim any untidy edges with scissors and keep warm. Cook the remaining eggs in the same way.

5 To serve, spoon the spinach on to warmed plates and make an indentation in each mound. Place the eggs on top and pour over a little hollandaise sauce. Serve the remaining hollandaise separately.

ASPARAGUS WITH ORANGE SAUCE

The white asparagus grown in France is considered a delicacy by many, although it doesn't have the intense flavour of the green. White and large green spears are best peeled before cooking.

Preparation time 2–3 minutes
Cooking time 15 minutes

SERVES 6
175g/6oz/ ¾ cup unsalted
*   butter, diced*
3 egg yolks
15ml/1 tbsp cold water
15ml/1 tbsp fresh lemon juice
grated rind and juice of
*   1 unwaxed orange, plus extra*
*   shreds of orange rind,*
*   to garnish*
salt and cayenne pepper, to taste
30–36 thick asparagus spears

1 Melt the butter in a small saucepan over a low heat; do not boil. Skim off any foam and set the pan aside.

2 In a heatproof bowl set over a saucepan of barely simmering water or in the top of a double boiler, whisk together the egg yolks, water, lemon juice and 15ml/1 tbsp of the orange juice. Season with salt. Place the saucepan or double boiler over a very low heat and whisk constantly until the mixture begins to thicken and the whisk begins to leave tracks on the base of the pan. Remove the pan from the heat.

3 Whisk in the melted butter, drop by drop until the sauce begins to thicken, then pour it in a little more quickly, leaving behind the milky solids at the bottom of the pan. Whisk in the orange rind and 30–60ml/2–4 tbsp of the orange juice. Season with salt and cayenne and keep warm, stirring occasionally

4 Cut off the tough ends from the asparagus spears and trim to the same length. If peeling, hold each spear gently by the tip, then use a vegetable peeler to strip off the peel and scales from just below the tip to the end. Rinse in cold water.

5 Pour water to a depth of 5cm/2in into a large deep frying pan or wok and bring to the boil over a medium-high heat. Add the asparagus and bring back to the boil, then simmer for 4–7 minutes, until just tender.

6 Carefully transfer the spears to a large colander to drain, then lay them on a dish towel; pat dry. Arrange on a large serving platter or individual plates and spoon over a little sauce. Scatter the orange rind over the sauce and serve at once.

COOK'S TIP
This sauce is a kind of hollandaise and needs gentle treatment. If the egg yolk mixture thickens too quickly, remove from the heat and plunge the base of the pan or bowl into cold water to prevent the sauce from curdling. The sauce should keep over hot water for 1 hour, but don't let it get too hot.

ASPARAGUS ROLLS WITH HERB BUTTER SAUCE

For a taste sensation, try tender asparagus spears wrapped in crisp filo pastry. The buttery herb sauce doesn't take long to make and is the perfect accompaniment.

Preparation time 5 minutes
Cooking time 8 minutes

SERVES 2

4 sheets of filo pastry
50g/2oz/ ¼ cup butter, melted
16 young asparagus spears, trimmed
mixed salad, to garnish

For the sauce
2 shallots, finely chopped
1 bay leaf
150ml/ ¼ pint/ ⅔ cup dry white wine
175g/6oz/ ¾ cup butter, melted
15ml/1 tbsp chopped fresh herbs
salt and ground black pepper
snipped chives, to garnish

1 Preheat the oven to 200ºC/ 400ºF/Gas 6. Grease a baking sheet. Brush each filo sheet with melted butter. Fold one corner of the sheet down to the bottom edge to give a wedge shape.

COOK'S TIPS
Make miniature asparagus rolls for parties. Cut smaller rectangles of filo and roll around a single asparagus spear. Serve hot, with the suggested sauce, or cold, with a light mayonnaise. For a quicker and more economical version, use well-drained canned asparagus cuts, folding them inside filo envelopes.

2 Lay 4 asparagus spears on top at the longest edge and roll up towards the shortest edge. Using the remaining filo and asparagus spears, make 3 more rolls in the same way.

3 Lay the rolls on the prepared baking sheet. Brush with the remaining melted butter. Bake in the oven for 8 minutes until golden.

4 Meanwhile, make the sauce. Put the shallots, bay leaf and wine into a pan. Cover and cook over a high heat until the wine is reduced to about 45–60ml/3–4 tbsp.

5 Strain the wine mixture into a heatproof bowl. Whisk in the butter, a little at a time, until the sauce is smooth and glossy.

6 Stir in the herbs and add salt and pepper to taste. Keep the sauce warm over a pan of barely simmering water. Serve the rolls on individual plates with the salad garnish. Serve the butter sauce separately, sprinkled with a few snipped chives.

EGG AND TOMATO SALAD WITH CRAB

Preparation time 5 minutes
Cooking time Nil

SERVES 4
1 round lettuce
2 x 200g/7oz cans crabmeat, drained
4 hard-boiled eggs, sliced
16 cherry tomatoes, halved
½ green pepper, seeded and
thinly sliced
6 stoned black olives, sliced
For the dressing
250ml/8fl oz/1 cup mayonnaise
10ml/2 tsp fresh lemon juice
45ml/3 tbsp chilli sauce
½ green pepper, seeded and
finely chopped
5ml/1 tsp creamed horseradish
5ml/1 tsp Worcestershire sauce

1 To make the dressing, place all the ingredients in a bowl and mix well. Set aside in a cool place.

2 Line four plates with the lettuce leaves. Mound the crabmeat in the centre. Arrange the eggs around the outside with the tomatoes on top.

3 Spoon some of the dressing over the crabmeat. Arrange the green pepper slices on top and sprinkle with the olives. Serve with the remaining dressing.

SUMMER TUNA SALAD

This colourful salad is perfect for a summer lunch in the garden – use canned or freshly cooked salmon in place of the tuna, if you like.

Preparation time 20 minutes
Cooking time Nil

SERVES 4–6
175g/6oz radishes
1 cucumber
3 celery sticks
1 yellow pepper
175g/6oz cherry tomatoes, halved
4 spring onions, thinly sliced
45ml/3 tbsp fresh lemon juice
45ml/3 tbsp olive oil
2 x 200g/7oz cans tuna, drained
and flaked
30ml/2 tbsp chopped fresh parsley
salt and ground black pepper
lettuce leaves, to serve
thin strips of twisted lemon rind,
to garnish

1 Cut the radishes, cucumber, celery and yellow pepper into small cubes. Place in a large, shallow dish with the cherry tomatoes and spring onions.

2 Put the lemon juice in a bowl. Whisk in the oil, with salt and pepper to taste. Add the dressing to the vegetables, toss to coat, then set aside for 15 minutes.

3 Add the flaked tuna and parsley to the mixture and toss gently until well combined.

4 Arrange the lettuce leaves on a platter and spoon the salad into the centre. Garnish with the twisted lemon rind.

VARIATION
Prepare the vegetables as suggested in the recipe and add the chopped parsley. Arrange lettuce leaves on individual plates and divide the vegetable mixture among them. Place a mound of tuna on top of each and finish with a dollop of mayonnaise.

SALADE NIÇOISE

Preparation and
cooking time 20 minutes

SERVES 4
90ml/6 tbsp olive oil
30ml/2 tbsp tarragon vinegar
5ml/1 tsp tarragon or Dijon mustard
1 small garlic clove, crushed
115g/4oz French beans
12 small new or salad potatoes
3–4 Little Gem lettuces
200g/7oz can tuna in oil, drained
6 anchovy fillets, halved lengthways
12 stoned black olives
4 tomatoes, chopped
4 spring onions, finely chopped
10ml/2 tsp capers
30ml/2 tbsp pine nuts
2 hard-boiled eggs, chopped
salt and ground black pepper

1 Mix the oil, vinegar, mustard, garlic and seasoning with a wooden spoon in a large salad bowl.

COOK'S TIP
When buying the potatoes, pick the smallest ones you can find, so that they cook quickly.

2 Cook the French beans and potatoes in separate pans of boiling salted water until just tender. Drain and add to the bowl with the lettuce, tuna, anchovies, olives, tomatoes, spring onions and capers.

3 Toast the pine nuts in a small frying pan over a medium heat until lightly browned.

4 Sprinkle the pine nuts over the salad while they are still hot, add the chopped hard-boiled eggs and toss all the ingredients together well. Serve at once, with chunks of hot crusty bread.

AVOCADO AND PAPAYA SALAD

Preparation time 6–8 minutes
Cooking time Nil

SERVES 4

2 ripe avocados
1 ripe papaya
1 large orange
1 small red onion
25–50g/1–2oz small rocket leaves or
*   lamb's lettuce*
For the dressing
60ml/4 tbsp olive oil
30ml/2 tbsp fresh lemon or lime juice
salt and ground black pepper

1 Halve the avocados and remove the stones. Carefully peel off the skin, then slice each avocado half thickly.

2 Peel the papaya. Cut it in half lengthways and scoop out the seeds with a spoon. Set aside about 5ml/1 tsp of the seeds for the dressing. Cut each half into eight slices.

3 Peel the orange. Using a small sharp knife, cut out the segments, cutting either side of the dividing membranes. Slice the onion thinly and separate into rings.

4 Make the dressing. Combine the oil, lemon or lime juice and seasoning in a bowl and mix well. Stir in the reserved papaya seeds.

5 Assemble the salad on four individual serving plates. Alternate slices of papaya and avocado. Add the orange segments and a mound of rocket or lamb's lettuce topped with onion rings. Spoon over the dressing and serve.

CORNED BEEF AND EGG HASH

This classic American hash is made with corned beef and is a popular brunch or lunchtime dish.

Preparation time 4 minutes
Cooking time 12–14 minutes

Serves 4

30ml/2 tbsp sunflower oil
25g/1oz/2 tbsp butter
1 onion, finely chopped
1 small green pepper, seeded and diced
2 large boiled potatoes, diced
350g/12oz can corned beef, cubed
1.5ml/ ¼ tsp grated nutmeg
1.5ml/ ¼ tsp paprika
4 eggs
salt and ground black pepper
chopped fresh parsley, to garnish
sweet chilli sauce or tomato sauce, to serve

1 Heat the oil and butter together in a large frying pan and add the onion. Fry for 5–6 minutes, until softened.

2 In a bowl, mix together the pepper, potatoes, corned beef, nutmeg and paprika and season well. Add to the pan and toss gently. Press down lightly and fry over a medium heat for about 3–4 minutes, until a golden brown crust has formed on the bottom.

3 Stir the hash mixture through to distribute the crust, then repeat the frying twice, until the mixture is well browned.

4 Make four wells in the hash and crack an egg into each. Cover. Poach until the whites are just set.

5 Sprinkle with chopped parsley and cut the hash into quarters. Serve hot with sweet chilli sauce or tomato sauce.

STILTON BEEFBURGERS

Rather more up-market than the traditional beefburger, this tasty recipe contains a delicious surprise. The lightly melted Stilton cheese encased in this crunchy beefburger is absolutely delicious.

Preparation time 5 minutes
Cooking time 10 minutes

SERVES 4

450g/1lb/2 cups minced beef
1 onion, finely chopped
1 celery stick, chopped
5ml/1 tsp dried mixed herbs
5ml/1 tsp prepared mustard
50g/2oz/ 1/2 cup crumbled blue
   Stilton cheese
4 burger buns
salt and ground black pepper

 1 Place the minced beef in a bowl together with the onion and celery. Season well.

2 Stir in the herbs and mustard, bringing the mixture together to form a firm mixture.

3 Divide the mixture into eight equal portions. Place four on a chopping board and flatten each one slightly to make patties.

4 Place the crumbled cheese in the centre of each patty.

5 Flatten the remaining mixture and place on top. Mould the mixture together, encasing the crumbled cheese and shape into four neat burgers. Preheat the grill.

6 Grill under a medium heat for 10 minutes, turning once or until cooked through. Split the burger buns and place a burger inside each. Serve with salad and mustard pickle or tomato ketchup, if liked, although neither is essential, with the Stilton for flavouring.

VEAL KIDNEYS WITH MUSTARD

In France, where this recipe originated, veal kidneys are easily found, but this dish is equally delicious made with lamb's kidneys.

Preparation time 5 minutes
Cooking time 10–12 minutes

SERVES 4

2 veal kidneys or 8–10 lamb's kidneys, trimmed and membranes removed
25g/1oz/2 tbsp butter
15ml/1 tbsp vegetable oil
115g/4oz/1 cup button mushrooms, quartered
60ml/4 tbsp chicken stock
30ml/2 tbsp brandy (optional)
175ml/6fl oz/ ¾ cup crème fraîche or double cream
30ml/2 tbsp Dijon mustard
salt and ground black pepper
snipped fresh chives, to garnish

1 Cut the veal kidneys into pieces, discarding any fat. If using lamb's kidneys, remove the central core by cutting a V-shape from the middle of each kidney. Cut each kidney into three or four pieces.

COOK'S TIP
Be sure not to cook the sauce too long once the mustard is added or it will lose its piquancy.

2 In a large frying pan, melt the butter with the oil over a high heat and swirl to blend. Add the kidneys and sauté for 3–4 minutes, stirring frequently, until browned, then transfer them to a plate using a slotted spoon.

3 Add the mushrooms to the pan and sauté for 2–3 minutes until golden, stirring frequently. Pour in the chicken stock and brandy, if using, then bring to the boil and boil for 2 minutes.

4 Lower the heat, stir in the crème fraîche or double cream and cook for about 2–3 minutes until the sauce is slightly thickened. Stir in the mustard and season with salt and pepper, then add the kidneys and cook for 1 minute to reheat. Spoon into a serving dish, scatter over the chives and serve.

BEEF STRIPS WITH ORANGE AND GINGER

Stir-frying is one of the best ways to cook with the minimum of fat. It's also one of the quickest ways to cook, provided you choose tender meat.

Preparation time 15 minutes
Cooking time 5 minutes

SERVES 4
*450g/1lb lean beef rump, fillet or
 sirloin, cut into thin strips
grated rind and juice of 1 orange
15ml/1 tbsp light soy sauce
5ml/1 tsp cornflour
2.5cm/1in piece of fresh root ginger,
 finely chopped
15ml/1 tbsp sunflower oil
1 large carrot, cut into thin strips
2 spring onions, thinly sliced
noodles or rice, to serve*

 1 Place the beef strips in a bowl and sprinkle over the orange rind and juice. If possible, leave to marinate for 10 minutes, or up to 30 minutes if you can spare the time.

2 Drain the liquid from the meat and set aside, then mix the meat with the soy sauce, cornflour, and ginger.

> **COOK'S TIP**
> Just before serving, toss the stir-fry with 5ml/1 tsp sesame oil. If you haven't any sesame oil, use flavoured chilli oil, or a nut oil, such as hazelnut or walnut.

3 Heat the oil in a wok or large frying pan and add the beef. Stir-fry for 1 minute until lightly coloured, then add the carrot and stir-fry for another 2–3 minutes more.

4 Stir in the spring onions and reserved liquid, then cook, stirring, until boiling and thickened. Serve hot with noodles or rice.

RAGOUT OF VEAL

Full of flavour, this is quick and easy. Use small cubes of pork fillet if you prefer.

Preparation time 3 minutes
Cooking time 17 minutes

SERVES 4
450g/1lb veal fillet or loin
30ml/2 tbsp olive oil
10–12 tiny onions, kept whole
1 yellow pepper, seeded and cut
* in eight*
1 orange or red pepper, seeded and
* cut in eight*
3 plum tomatoes, peeled and
* quartered*
4 sprigs of fresh basil
30ml/2 tbsp dry martini or sherry
salt and ground black pepper

1 Trim off any fat and cut the veal into cubes. Heat the oil in a frying pan and gently fry the veal and onions until browned.

2 After a couple of minutes add the peppers and tomatoes. Fry for another 4 minutes.

3 Add half the basil leaves, roughly chopped, the martini or sherry, and seasoning. Cook, stirring frequently, for 10 minutes or until the meat is tender.

4 Sprinkle with the remaining basil leaves and serve hot.

LAMB'S LIVER WITH PEPPERS

Tender and tasty lamb's liver can be fried with all sorts of ingredients. Here it is matched with peppers and peppercorns.

Preparation time 7 minutes
Cooking time 3–4 minutes

SERVES 4
30ml/2 tbsp olive oil
2 shallots, sliced
450g/1lb lamb's liver, cut in
* thin strips*
1 garlic clove, crushed
10ml/2 tsp green peppercorns,
* crushed (or more to taste)*
¹/₂ red pepper, seeded and cut in strips
¹/₂ orange or yellow pepper, seeded
* and cut in strips*
30ml/2 tbsp crème fraîche
salt and ground black pepper
rice or noodles, to serve

COOK'S TIP
Lamb's liver is best when still very slightly pink in the middle. Watch it closely as it soon overcooks.

1 Heat the oil and fry the shallots briskly for 1 minute. Add the liver, garlic, peppercorns and peppers, then stir-fry for 3–4 minutes.

2 Stir in the crème fraîche, season to taste and serve immediately with rice or noodles.

LAMB CHOPS WITH MINT VINAIGRETTE

Serving vinaigrette sauces with meat came in with nouvelle cuisine and stayed. This one offers a classic combination — lamb and mint — in a new style.

Preparation time 4 minutes
Cooking time 6–7 minutes

Serves 4

8 loin lamb chops or 4 double loin
  chops, about 2cm/³⁄₄ in thick
coarsely ground black pepper
fresh mint, to garnish
sautéed potatoes, to serve
For the mint vinaigrette
30ml/2 tbsp white wine vinegar
2.5ml/ ¹⁄₂ tsp clear honey
1 small garlic clove, very
  finely chopped
60ml/4 tbsp extra virgin olive oil
20g/ ³⁄₄oz/ ¹⁄₂ cup fresh mint leaves,
  finely chopped
1 ripe plum tomato, peeled, seeded
  and finely diced
salt and ground black pepper

1 To make the vinaigrette, put the vinegar, honey, garlic, salt and pepper in a small bowl and whisk thoroughly to combine.

3 Put the lamb chops on a board and trim off any excess fat. Sprinkle with the pepper and press on to both sides of the meat.

2 Slowly whisk in the oil, then stir in the mint and tomato and set aside.

4 Lightly oil a heavy cast iron griddle and set over a high heat until very hot but not smoking. Place the chops on the griddle and reduce the heat to medium. Cook the chops for 6–7 minutes, turning once, or until done as preferred (medium-rare meat will still be slightly soft when pressed, medium will be springy and well-done firm). Serve the chops with the vinaigrette and sautéed potatoes, garnished with mint.

COOK'S TIP
The chops can also be grilled under a preheated grill or barbecued over char-coal until done as you like. If barbecu-ing, put them in a hinged wire grill to make them easier to turn.

PORK WITH MARSALA AND JUNIPER

Although most frequently used in desserts, Sicilian marsala gives savoury dishes a rich, fruity and alcoholic tang. Use good quality butcher's pork, which won't be overwhelmed by the intense flavour of the sauce.

Preparation time 4 minutes
Cooking time 15–16 minutes

SERVES 4

25g/1oz/ ½ cup dried cep or
   porcini mushrooms
4 pork escalopes
10ml/2 tsp balsamic vinegar
8 garlic cloves
15g/ ½oz/1 tbsp butter
45ml/3 tbsp marsala
several fresh rosemary sprigs
10 juniper berries, crushed
salt and ground black pepper
noodles and green vegetables, to serve

1 Put the dried mushrooms in a bowl and just cover with hot water. Leave to stand.

2 Place the pork escalopes on a board, brush with 5ml/1 tsp of the vinegar and add a generous and even grinding of salt and black pepper. Bring a small saucepan of water to the boil and add the garlic cloves. Cook for 10 minutes until soft. Drain, put the garlic in a bowl and set aside while you cook the pork escalopes.

3 Melt the butter in a large frying pan. Add the pork and fry quickly until browned on the underside. Turn the meat over and cook for another minute.

4 Add the marsala and rosemary to the pan. Drain the dried mushrooms, saving the juices, and add them to the mixture. Stir in 60ml/4 tbsp of the mushroom juices, then add the garlic cloves, juniper berries and remaining vinegar.

5 Simmer the mixture gently for about 3 minutes until the pork is cooked. Season lightly and serve hot with noodles and vegetables.

COOK'S TIP
Juniper berries are the principal flavouring for gin. When added to meat, they impart a gamey flavour.

SWEET-AND-SOUR PORK, THAI-STYLE

Sweet and sour is traditionally a Chinese creation, but the Thais do it very well. This version has a clean, fresh flavour.

Preparation time 6 minutes
Cooking time 12–14 minutes

SERVES 4

350g/12oz lean pork
30ml/2 tbsp vegetable oil
4 garlic cloves, finely sliced
1 small red onion, sliced
30ml/2 tbsp fish sauce
15ml/1 tbsp granulated sugar
1 red pepper, seeded and diced
1/2 cucumber, seeded and sliced
2 plum tomatoes, cut into wedges
2 spring onions, cut into short lengths
115g/4oz pineapple, cut into
    small chunks
ground black pepper
fresh coriander leaves and shredded
    spring onions, to garnish

1 | Slice the pork into thin strips. Heat the oil in a wok or pan.

2 | Fry the garlic until golden, then add the pork and stir-fry for about 4–5 minutes. Add the onion.

3 | Season the meat and onion mixture with fish sauce, sugar and ground black pepper. Stir the mixture (or toss it over the heat with two spoons or spatulas) for about 4 minutes until the pork is cooked.

4 | Add the rest of the vegetables, with the pineapple. You may need to add a few tablespoons of water. Stir-fry for 3–4 minutes more. Serve hot, garnished with coriander leaves and spring onion.

CHICKEN CHOW MEIN

Chow Mein is arguably the best known Chinese noodle dish in the West.

Preparation time 4–5 minutes
Cooking time 14 minutes

SERVES 4
350g/12oz noodles
225g/8oz skinless, boneless
  chicken breasts
45ml/3 tbsp soy sauce
15ml/1 tbsp rice wine or dry sherry
15ml/1 tbsp dark sesame oil
60ml/4 tbsp vegetable oil
2 garlic cloves, finely chopped
50g/2oz mangetouts, topped
  and tailed
115g/4oz beansprouts
50g/2oz ham, finely shredded
4 spring onions, finely chopped
salt and ground black pepper

1 Cook the noodles in a large saucepan of boiling lightly salted water until tender.

2 Meanwhile, slice the chicken into fine shreds about 5cm/2in in length. Place in a bowl and add 10ml/2 tsp of the soy sauce, the rice wine or sherry and sesame oil.

3 Heat half the vegetable oil in a wok or large frying pan over a high heat. When it starts smoking, add the chicken mixture. Stir-fry for 2 minutes, then transfer the chicken to a plate and keep it hot.

4 Wipe the wok clean and heat the remaining oil. Stir in the garlic, mangetouts, beansprouts and shredded ham. Stir-fry for 2–3 minutes more over a high heat.

5 Drain the noodles, rinse them under cold water, then drain them again. Pat them dry with kitchen paper and add to the wok. Continue to stir-fry until the noodles are heated through. Add the remaining soy sauce and season with salt and ground black pepper. Return the chicken and any juices to the noodle mixture, add the chopped spring onions and give the mixture a final stir. Serve at once.

Caribbean Chicken Kebabs

These quick-to-cook kebabs have a rich, sunshine Caribbean flavour and the marinade keeps them moist without the need for oil.

Preparation time 12 minutes
Cooking time 8 minutes

Serves 4
*500g/1¼ lb skinless, boneless
  chicken breasts
finely grated rind of 1 lime
30ml/2 tbsp lime juice
15ml/1 tbsp rum
15ml/1 tbsp light soft
  brown sugar
15ml/1 tsp ground cinnamon
2 mangoes, peeled and cubed
rice and salad, to serve*

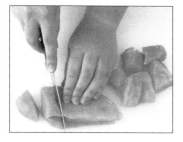

1 Cut the chicken into bite-size chunks and place in a bowl with the lime rind and juice, rum, sugar and cinnamon. Toss well and set aside for 10 minutes.

2 Drain the chicken, saving the juices and thread it on to four skewers, alternating with the mango cubes.

3 Cook the skewers under a grill, or on a barbecue, for about 8 minutes, turning occasionally and basting with the juices, until the chicken is tender and golden brown. Serve the kebabs at once, with rice and salad.

COOK'S TIP
The rum or sherry adds a lovely rich flavour to the marinade, but it can be omitted if you prefer to avoid the added alcohol.

VARIATIONS
Try other fruits in place of the mangoes – chunks of fresh pineapple or firm peaches or nectarines would be equally good in this recipe.

CAJUN-SPICED CHICKEN

Preparation time 2 minutes
Cooking time 10–15 minutes

SERVES 6

6 medium skinless boneless
   chicken breasts
75g/3oz/¹/₃ cup butter
5ml/1 tsp garlic powder
10ml/2 tsp onion powder
5ml/2 tsp cayenne pepper
10ml/2 tsp paprika
1.5ml/¹/₄ tsp ground cumin
5ml/1 tsp dried thyme
salt and ground black pepper
salad leaves and pepper strips,
   to garnish

1   Slice each chicken breast in
    half horizontally, making two
pieces of about the same thickness.
Flatten them slightly with the heel of
your hand.

2   Put the butter in a small
    saucepan and melt over a low
heat. Do not let it brown.

VARIATION

For Cajun-spiced Fish, substitute six
white fish fillets for the chicken. Do not
slice the fish fillets in half, but
season as for the chicken breasts and
cook for about 2 minutes on one side
and 1¹/₂–2 minutes on the other, until
the fish flakes easily when tested with
the tip of a sharp knife.

3   Mix the remaining ingredients
    in a bowl, adding 7.5ml/1¹/₂ tsp
each of salt and pepper. Brush the
chicken on both sides with a little of
the melted butter. Sprinkle evenly
with the seasoning mixture.

4   Heat a large heavy-based frying
    pan over a high heat for about
5–8 minutes, until a drop of water
sprinkled on the surface sizzles.

5   Drizzle 5ml/1 tsp melted butter
    on to each chicken piece.
Place them in the frying pan in an
even layer, two or three at a time,
and cook for 2–3 minutes, until the
underside begins to blacken. Turn
the chicken over and cook the other
side for 2–3 minutes more. Remove
from the pan and keep hot while
cooking successive batches. Serve hot
with salad leaves and pepper strips.

WARM CHICKEN AND VEGETABLE SALAD

Succulent cooked chicken pieces are combined with vegetables in a light chilli dressing.

Preparation time 7 minutes
Cooking time 10 minutes

SERVES 6

50g/2oz mixed salad leaves
50g/2oz baby spinach leaves
50g/2oz watercress
30ml/2 tbsp chilli sauce
30ml/2 tbsp dry sherry
15ml/1 tbsp light soy sauce
15ml/1 tbsp tomato ketchup
10ml/2 tsp olive oil
8 shallots, finely chopped
1 garlic clove, crushed
350g/12oz skinless, boneless chicken
    breast, cut into thin strips
1 red pepper, seeded and sliced
175g/6oz/1½ cups mangetouts
400g/14oz can baby corn, drained
    and halved
275g/10oz can brown rice
salt and ground black pepper
fresh parsley sprig, to garnish

1 Tear any large salad leaves into smaller pieces. Arrange, with the spinach leaves, on a serving dish. Add the watercress and toss to mix.

2 In a small bowl, mix together the chilli sauce, dry sherry, light soy sauce and tomato ketchup and set aside.

3 Heat the oil in a large non-stick frying pan or wok. Add the shallots and garlic and stir-fry over a medium heat for 1 minute.

4 Add the chicken and stir-fry for 3–4 minutes, then add the pepper, mangetouts, baby corn and rice and stir-fry for 2–3 minutes more.

5 Pour in the chilli sauce mixture and stir-fry for 2–3 minutes, until hot and bubbling. Season to taste. Spoon the chicken mixture over the salad leaves, toss together to mix and serve immediately, garnished with fresh parsley.

COOK'S TIP
Use other lean meat, such as turkey breast, or lean cuts of beef or pork, in place of the chicken. You could also use prawns. If using cooked prawns, add them to the pan with the chilli sauce so they are not overcooked.

TURKEY WITH YELLOW PEPPER SAUCE

Preparation time 6–8 minutes
Cooking time 12 minutes

Serves 4
30ml/2 tbsp olive oil
2 large yellow peppers, seeded
  and chopped
1 small onion, chopped
15ml/1 tbsp freshly squeezed
  orange juice
300ml/ ¹/₂ pint/1¹/₄ cups chicken stock
4 turkey escalopes
75g/3oz Boursin or garlicky
  cream cheese
16 fresh basil leaves
25g/1oz/2 tbsp butter
salt and ground black pepper

1 To make the sauce, heat half the oil in a pan and gently fry the peppers and onion until beginning to soften. Add the orange juice and stock and cook until very soft. Meanwhile, lay the turkey escalopes between sheets of clear film and beat them out lightly.

2 Spread the turkey escalopes with the Boursin or garlicky cream cheese. Chop half the basil and sprinkle on top, then roll up, tucking in the ends like an envelope. Secure with half a cocktail stick.

3 Heat the remaining oil and the butter in a frying pan and fry the escalopes for 7–8 minutes, turning them frequently, until golden and cooked.

4 While the escalopes are cooking, press the pepper mixture through a sieve, or blend until smooth, then strain back into the pan. Season to taste and warm through, or serve cold, with the escalopes, garnished with the remaining basil leaves.

COOK'S TIP
Chicken breast fillets or veal escalopes could be used in place of the turkey, if you prefer.

COD WITH CAPER SAUCE

The quick and easy sauce with a slightly sharp and nutty flavour is a very effective way of enhancing this simple fish.

Preparation time 2 minutes
Cooking time 10 minutes

SERVES 4

4 cod steaks, about 175g/6oz each
115g/4oz/¹/₂ cup butter
15ml/1 tbsp small capers, rinsed,
*   plus 15ml/1 tbsp vinegar from the*
*   caper jar*
15ml/1 tbsp chopped fresh parsley
salt and ground black pepper
fresh tarragon sprigs, to garnish

1 Preheat the grill. Season the cod. Melt 25g/1oz/2 tbsp of the butter, then brush some over one side of each piece of cod.

2 Grill the cod for 4 minutes, turn the fish over, then brush with melted butter and cook for a further 4–5 minutes, or until the fish flakes easily.

3 Meanwhile, heat the remaining butter until it turns golden brown, then add the vinegar followed by the capers and stir well.

4 Pour the vinegar, butter and capers over the fish, sprinkle with parsley and garnish with the tarragon sprigs.

VARIATIONS

Thick tail fillets of cod or haddock could be used in place of the cod steaks. The sauce is also excellent with skate that has been pan-fried in butter.

TAGLIATELLE WITH SAFFRON MUSSELS

Preparation time 6 minutes
Cooking time 14 minutes

SERVES 4

1.75 kg/4–4¹/₂lb live mussels
150ml/ ¹/₄ pint/ ²/₃ cup dry white wine
2 shallots, chopped
350g/12oz fresh or dried tagliatelle
25g/1oz/2 tbsp butter
2 garlic cloves, crushed
250ml/8fl oz/1 cup double cream
generous pinch of saffron strands
1 egg yolk
salt and ground black pepper
30ml/2 tbsp chopped fresh parsley,
*   to garnish*

1 Scrub the mussels well under cold running water. Remove the beards and discard any mussels that are open.

2 Place the mussels in a large pan with the wine and shallots. Cover and cook over a high heat, shaking occasionally, for 5–8 minutes until the mussels have opened. Drain the mussels, reserving the liquid. Discard any mussels that remain closed. Shell most of the mussels; keep warm.

3 Bring the reserved cooking liquid to the boil, then reduce by half. Strain into a jug.

4 Cook the tagliatelle in a large pan of boiling salted water until just tender. Meanwhile, melt the butter in a separate pan and fry the garlic for about a minute. Pour in the reserved mussel liquid, cream and saffron strands. Heat gently until the sauce thickens slightly. Remove the pan from the heat and stir in the egg yolk, shelled mussels and seasoning to taste.

5 Drain the tagliatelle, transfer to warmed serving bowls, then spoon the sauce over and sprinkle with chopped parsley. Garnish with the mussels in shells. Serve at once.

COD CREOLE

Preparation time 5 minutes
Cooking time 10 minutes

SERVES 4

450g/1lb cod fillets, skinned
15ml/1 tbsp lime or lemon juice
10ml/2 tsp olive oil
1 medium onion, finely chopped
1 green pepper, seeded and sliced
2.5ml/ ½ tsp cayenne pepper
2.5ml/ ½ tsp garlic salt
400g/14oz can chopped tomatoes

COOK'S TIP
Be careful not to overcook the fish –
or to let it bubble too vigorously in the
sauce – or the chunks will break up.
Test the fish frequently, and remove it
from the heat the moment it is cooked.

1 Cut the cod fillets into bite-size
chunks and sprinkle with the
lime or lemon juice.

2 In a large pan, heat the olive
oil and sauté the onion and
pepper gently until softened. Add the
cayenne pepper and garlic salt.

3 Stir in the cod chunks with the
chopped tomatoes. Bring to a
boil, then cover and simmer for about
5 minutes, or until the fish flakes easily
when tested with the tip of a sharp
knife. Serve with boiled rice or potatoes.

FIVE-SPICE FISH

*Chinese mixtures of spicy, sweet and
sour flavours are great with fish.*

Preparation time 8 minutes
Cooking time 6 minutes

SERVES 4

*4 white fish fillets, such as cod,
haddock, whiting or hoki, about
175g/6oz each*
5ml/1 tsp Chinese five-spice powder
20ml/4 tsp cornflour
15ml/1 tbsp sunflower oil
3 spring onions, shredded
5ml/1 tsp grated fresh root ginger
*150g/5oz/1¼ cups button
mushrooms, sliced*
115g/4oz/ ⅔ cup baby corn, sliced
30ml/2 tbsp soy sauce
45ml/3 tbsp dry sherry
5ml/1 tsp granulated ground sugar
salt and ground black pepper

1 Toss the fish in the five-spice
powder and cornflour to coat.

2 Heat the oil in a frying pan
or wok and stir-fry the spring
onions, ginger, mushrooms and corn
for 1 minute. Add the spiced fish and
cook for 2 minutes, turning once.

3 Mix together the soy sauce,
sherry and sugar, then pour
over the fish. Simmer for 2 minutes.
Season to taste. Serve with noodles
and stir-fried vegetables.

COOK'S TIP
Chinese noodles are available in most
large supermarkets and make a very
speedy accompaniment since they only
need to be soaked in boiling water for
a few minutes before being drained
and served.

FISH BALLS IN TOMATO SAUCE

This quick meal is a good choice for young children, as you can be sure there are no bones.

Preparation time 4 minutes
Cooking time 14 minutes

SERVES 4

*450g/1lb white fish fillets, such as
    haddock or cod, skinned*
*60ml/4 tbsp fresh wholemeal
    breadcrumbs*
30ml/2 tbsp snipped fresh chives
400g/14oz can chopped tomatoes
*50g/2oz/ ¹/₂ cup button mushrooms,
    sliced*
salt and ground black pepper

1 Cut the fish fillets into large chunks and place in a food processor. Add the wholemeal breadcrumbs and chives. Season to taste with salt and pepper, and process until the fish is finely chopped, but still has some texture.

2 Divide the fish mixture into about 16 even-size pieces, then mould them into balls.

3 Place the tomatoes and mushrooms in a wide saucepan and cook over a medium heat until boiling. Add the fish balls, cover and simmer for about 10 minutes, until cooked. Serve hot.

COOK'S TIPS
Instead of using a can of chopped tomatoes and fresh mushrooms, you could substitute a jar of ready-made tomato and mushroom sauce. Just add the fish balls and simmer for about 10 minutes. When making this dish for young children, try cooking the fish balls in their favourite canned tomato soup – even children who normally turn up their noses at anything other than fish and chips will love it.

MACKEREL KEBABS WITH PARSLEY DRESSING

Oily fish, such as mackerel, are ideal for grilling as they cook quickly and need no extra oil.

Preparation time 8 minutes
Cooking time 4 minutes

SERVES 4
450g/1lb mackerel fillets
finely grated rind and juice of
* 1 lemon*
45ml/3 tbsp chopped fresh parsley
16 cherry tomatoes
8 pitted black olives
salt and ground black pepper

1 Cut the fish into 4cm/1½in chunks and toss in a bowl with half the lemon rind and juice, half the parsley and some seasoning.

2 Preheat the grill. Thread the chunks of fish on to eight long wooden or metal skewers, alternating them with the cherry tomatoes and olives. Grill the kebabs for 3–4 minutes, turning the kebabs occasionally, until the fish is cooked.

3 Mix the remaining lemon rind and juice with the remaining parsley in a small bowl, then season to taste with salt and pepper. Spoon this dressing over the kebabs and serve hot, with plain boiled rice or noodles and a leafy green salad.

COOK'S TIP
When using wooden or bamboo kebab skewers, soak them in a bowl of cold water for 10 minutes to help prevent them from scorching.

VARIATIONS
Other firm-fleshed fish could be used in place of the mackerel – for a special occasion you could opt for salmon fillet or monkfish tail. Or try a mixture of the two, threading the fish chunks alternately on to the skewers with the tomatoes and olives.

SEAFOOD PILAFF

This all-in-one-pan main course is a satisfying and surprisingly quick and easy meal for any day of the week. For a special meal, substitute dry white wine for the orange juice.

Preparation time 3 minutes
Cooking time 17 minutes

SERVES 4
10ml/2 tsp olive oil
250g/9oz/1¼ cups long grain rice
5ml/1 tsp ground turmeric
1 red pepper, seeded and diced
1 small onion, finely chopped
2 courgettes, sliced
150g/5oz/1¼ cups button
  mushrooms, halved
350ml/12fl oz/1½ cups fish or
  chicken stock
150ml/¼ pint/⅔ cup orange juice
350g/12oz white fish fillets, skinned
  and cubed
12 cooked, shelled mussels
salt and ground black pepper
grated rind of 1 orange, to garnish

[1] Heat the oil in a large pan. Sauté the rice and ground turmeric over a low heat for about 1 minute.

[2] Add the pepper, onion, courgettes and mushrooms. Stir in the stock and orange juice. Bring to the boil.

[3] Reduce the heat and add the fish. Cover and simmer gently for about 15 minutes, until the rice is tender and the liquid absorbed. Stir in the mussels and heat thoroughly. Adjust the seasoning, sprinkle with orange rind, and serve hot.

COOK'S TIP
If you prefer, use fresh mussels in the shell. Scrub well and discard any that remain open. Add to the pan 5 minutes before the end of cooking. Throw away any mussels that have not opened after cooking.

SALMON PASTA WITH PARSLEY SAUCE

Preparation time 5 minutes
Cooking time 10–12 minutes

SERVES 4
450g/1lb salmon fillet, skinned
225g/8oz/2 cups dried pasta, such as
  penne or twists
175g/6oz cherry tomatoes, halved
150ml/¼ pint/⅔ cup low-fat
  crème fraîche
45ml/3 tbsp chopped fresh parsley
finely grated rind of ½ orange
salt and ground black pepper

COOK'S TIP
If you can't find low-fat crème fraîche, use ordinary crème fraîche or double cream instead.

[1] Cut the salmon into bite-size pieces, arrange on a heatproof plate, and cover with foil.

[2] Bring a large pan of salted water to the boil and add the pasta. Place the plate of salmon on top and cook for 10–12 minutes, until the pasta and salmon are cooked.

[3] Drain the pasta and toss with the tomatoes and salmon. Mix together the crème fraîche, parsley, orange rind and pepper to taste, then toss with the salmon and pasta and serve hot or cold.

WARM SALMON SALAD

Light and fresh, this salad should be served immediately, or you'll find the salad leaves will lose their bright colour and texture.

Preparation time 4–5 minutes
Cooking time 7 minutes

SERVES 4

450g/1lb salmon fillet, skinned
30ml/2 tbsp sesame oil
grated rind of ½ orange
juice of 1 orange
5ml/1 tsp Dijon mustard
15ml/1 tbsp chopped fresh tarragon
45ml/3 tbsp groundnut oil
115g/4oz fine green beans, trimmed
175g/6oz mixed salad leaves, such as
* young spinach leaves, radicchio,*
* frisée and oakleaf lettuce leaves*
15ml/1 tbsp toasted sesame seeds

1 Cut the salmon into bite-size pieces, then make the dressing. Mix together the sesame oil, orange rind and juice, mustard, chopped tarragon and seasoning in a bowl.

2 Heat the groundnut oil in a frying pan. Add the salmon pieces and fry for 3–4 minutes, until lightly browned but tender inside.

3 While the salmon is cooking, blanch the green beans in boiling salted water for 5–6 minutes, until crisp-tender.

4 Add the dressing to the salmon. Toss gently over the heat for 30 seconds. Remove from the heat.

5 Arrange the salad leaves on serving plates. Drain the beans and arrange on top. Spoon over the salmon and cooking juices and serve, sprinkled with the sesame seeds.

SALMON WITH WATERCRESS SAUCE

SERVES 4

300ml/¹/₂ pint/1¹/₄ cups crème
  fraîche
30ml/2 tbsp chopped fresh tarragon
25g/1oz/2 tbsp unsalted butter
15ml/1 tbsp sunflower oil
4 salmon fillets, skinned
1 garlic clove, crushed
120ml/4fl oz/ ¹/₂ cup dry white wine
1 bunch watercress
salt and ground black pepper

1 Gently heat the crème fraîche in a small pan until just beginning to boil. Remove the pan from the heat and stir in half the tarragon. Leave the herb cream to infuse while you cook the fish.

2 Heat the butter and oil in a frying pan, add the salmon and fry for 3–5 minutes on each side. Remove from the pan; keep hot.

3 Add the garlic; fry briefly, then add the wine and cook until reduced to 15ml/1 tbsp.

4 Meanwhile, strip the leaves off the watercress stalks and chop finely. Discard any damaged leaves.

5 Strain the herb cream into the pan and cook for a few minutes, stirring until the sauce has thickened. Stir in the remaining tarragon and the watercress. Cook for a few minutes. Season, spoon over the salmon and serve.

SPANISH-STYLE HAKE

*Cod and haddock steaks or cutlets
will work just as well as hake.*

Preparation time 3 minutes
Cooking time 15–16 minutes

SERVES 4

*30ml/2 tbsp olive oil
25g/1oz/2 tbsp butter
1 onion, chopped
3 garlic cloves, crushed
15ml/1 tbsp plain flour
2.5ml/ ½ tsp paprika
4 hake cutlets, about 175g/6oz each
250g/8oz fine green beans, chopped
350ml/12fl oz/1½ cups fish stock
150ml/ ¼ pint/ ⅔ cup dry white wine
30ml/2 tbsp dry sherry
16–20 live mussels, cleaned
45ml/3 tbsp chopped fresh parsley
salt and ground black pepper
crusty bread, to serve*

1 Heat the oil and butter in a
sauté or frying pan, add the
onion and cook for 5 minutes, until
softened, but not browned. Add the
garlic and cook for 1 minute more.

2 Mix together the plain flour and
paprika, then lightly dust over
the hake cutlets. Push the onion and
garlic to one side of the pan.

3 Add the hake cutlets to the pan
and fry until golden on both
sides. Stir in the beans, stock, wine,
sherry and seasoning. Bring to the
boil and cook for about 2 minutes.

4 Add the mussels and parsley,
cover the pan and cook until
the mussels have opened.

5 Discard any mussels that have
not opened, then serve the
hake in warmed soup bowls with
crusty bread to mop up the juices.

SPAGHETTI WITH SEAFOOD SAUCE

Preparation time 4 minutes
Cooking time 16 minutes

Serves 4

45ml/3 tbsp olive oil
1 medium onion, chopped
1 garlic clove, finely chopped
225g/8oz spaghetti
600ml/1 pint/2 ½ cups passata
15ml/1 tbsp tomato purée
5ml/1 tsp dried oregano
1 bay leaf
5ml/1 tsp granulated sugar
115g/4oz/1 cup cooked, peeled
  shrimps (rinsed well if canned)
115g/4oz/1 cup cooked,
  peeled prawns
175g/6oz/1½ cups cooked clam or
  cockle meat (rinsed well if canned
  or bottled)
15ml/1 tbsp lemon juice
45ml/3 tbsp chopped fresh parsley
25g/1oz/2 tbsp butter
salt and ground black pepper
4 whole cooked prawns, to garnish

1 Heat the oil in a pan and add the onion and garlic. Fry over a moderate heat for 5 minutes, until the onion has softened.

2 Meanwhile, cook the spaghetti in a large pan of boiling salted water for 10–12 minutes. Stir the passata, tomato purée, oregano, bay leaf and sugar into the onion mixture and season well. Bring to the boil, then lower the heat and simmer for 2–3 minutes.

3 Add the shellfish, lemon juice and half the parsley. Stir, cover and cook for 6–7 minutes.

4 Drain the spaghetti when it is just tender; add the butter to the pan. Return the drained spaghetti to the pan and toss in the butter until well coated. Season well.

5 Divide the spaghetti among four warmed plates and top with the seafood sauce. Sprinkle with the remaining chopped parsley, garnish with the whole prawns and serve immediately.

PAN-FRIED PRAWNS IN THEIR SHELLS

Although expensive, this is a very quick and simple dish, ideal for an impromptu supper with friends. Serve with hot crusty Italian bread to scoop up the juices.

Preparation time 2–3 minutes
Cooking time 5–8 minutes

SERVES 4
60ml/4 tbsp extra virgin olive oil
32 large raw prawns, in their shells
4 garlic cloves, finely chopped
120ml/4fl oz/ ½ cup Italian dry
  white vermouth
45ml/3 tbsp passata
salt and ground black pepper
chopped fresh flat leaf parsley,
  to garnish
crusty bread, to serve

1 Heat the olive oil in a large heavy-based frying pan until just sizzling. Add the prawns and toss over a medium to high heat until their shells just begin to turn pink. Sprinkle the garlic over the prawns in the pan and toss again, then add the vermouth and let it bubble, tossing the prawns constantly so that they cook evenly and absorb the flavours of the garlic and vermouth.

2 Keeping the pan on the heat, add the passata, with salt and pepper to taste. Stir until the prawns are thoroughly coated in the sauce. Serve at once, sprinkled with the parsley and accompanied by plenty of hot crusty bread.

GRILLED RED MULLET WITH ROSEMARY

This recipe is very simple – the taste of grilled red mullet is so good in itself that it needs very little to bring out the flavour.

Preparation time 10 minutes
Cooking time 10 minutes

SERVES 4
4 red mullet, cleaned, about
  275g/10oz each
4 garlic cloves, cut into thin slivers
75ml/5 tbsp olive oil
30ml/2 tbsp balsamic vinegar
10ml/2 tsp very finely chopped
  fresh rosemary
ground black pepper
coarse sea salt, to serve
fresh rosemary sprigs and lemon
  wedges, to garnish

1 Cut three diagonal slits in both sides of each fish. Push the garlic slivers into the slits. Place the fish in a single layer in a shallow dish. Whisk the oil, vinegar and rosemary in a bowl and add ground black pepper to taste.

VARIATION
Red mullet are extra delicious cooked on the barbecue. If possible, enclose them in a basket grill so that they are easy to turn over.

2 Pour the vinaigrette mixture over the fish, cover with clear film and set aside for 8 minutes, or longer if you can spare the time. Lift the fish out of the dish and put it on the rack of a grill pan. Reserve the marinade for basting.

3 Grill the fish for 5 minutes on each side, turning once and brushing with the marinade. Serve hot, sprinkled with coarse sea salt and garnished with fresh rosemary sprigs and lemon wedges.

MACKEREL WITH MUSTARD AND LEMON

Mackerel must be really fresh to be enjoyed. Look for bright, firm-looking fish.

Preparation time 5 minutes
Cooking time 10–12 minutes

SERVES 4

4 fresh mackerel, about 275g/10oz
  each, gutted and cleaned
175–225g/6–8oz young spinach
  leaves
For the mustard and lemon butter
115g/4oz/ ½ cup butter, melted
30ml/2 tbsp wholegrain mustard
grated rind of 1 lemon
30ml/2 tbsp lemon juice
45ml/3 tbsp chopped fresh parsley
salt and ground black pepper

1. Cut off the mackerel heads just behind the gills, using a sharp knife, then slit the belly so that each fish can be opened out flat.

2. Place the fish skin-side up. With the heel of your hand, press along the backbone to loosen it.

3. Turn the fish the right way up and pull the bone away. Cut off the tail and cut each fish in half lengthways. Wash and pat dry.

4. Score the skin three or four times, then season the fish. To make the mustard and lemon butter, mix together the melted butter, mustard, lemon rind and juice, parsley and seasoning. Place the mackerel on a grill rack. Brush a little of the butter over the mackerel and grill for 5 minutes each side, basting occasionally, until cooked through.

5. Arrange the spinach leaves in the centre of four large plates. Place the mackerel on top. Heat the remaining flavoured butter in a small pan until sizzling and pour over the mackerel. Serve at once.

PAN-STEAMED MUSSELS WITH THAI HERBS

Another simple and speedy dish. The lemon grass adds a refreshing tang.

Preparation time 5 minutes
Cooking time 5–7 minutes

SERVES 4–6

1kg/2 ¼ lb mussels, cleaned and
  beards removed
2 lemon grass stalks, finely chopped
4 shallots, chopped
4 kaffir lime leaves, roughly torn
2 red chillies, sliced
15ml/1 tbsp fish sauce
30ml/2 tbsp lime juice
chopped spring onions and coriander
  leaves, to garnish

 1 Place all the ingredients except the spring onions and coriander in a large pan. Stir well.

2 Cover the pan and place it over a medium-high heat. Steam for 5–7 minutes, shaking the saucepan occasionally, until the mussels open. Discard any mussels that do not open.

3 Lift out the cooked mussels with a slotted spoon and place on to a serving dish.

4 Garnish the mussels with the chopped spring onions and coriander leaves. Serve immediately.

CHILLI PRAWNS

This delightful, spicy combination makes a lovely light main course for a casual supper. Serve with rice, noodles or freshly cooked pasta and a leafy salad.

Preparation time 5 minutes
Cooking time 15 minutes

SERVES 3–4
45ml/3 tbsp olive oil
2 shallots, chopped
2 garlic cloves, chopped
1 red chilli, chopped
450g/1lb ripe tomatoes, peeled, seeded and chopped
15ml/1 tbsp tomato purée
1 bay leaf
1 thyme sprig
90ml/6 tbsp dry white wine
450g/1lb cooked, peeled large prawns
salt and ground black pepper
roughly torn basil leaves, to garnish

1 Heat the oil in a pan, then add the shallots, garlic and chilli. Fry until the garlic starts to brown.

2 Add the tomatoes, tomato purée, bay leaf, thyme, wine and seasoning. Bring to the boil, then reduce the heat and cook gently for about 10 minutes, stirring occasionally, until the sauce has thickened. Discard the herbs.

3 Stir the prawns into the sauce and heat through for a few minutes. Taste and adjust the seasoning. Scatter over the basil leaves and serve at once.

COOK'S TIP
For a milder flavour, remove all the seeds from the chilli.

SCALLOPS WITH GINGER

Scallops need little cooking, so are ideal for spontaneous suppers.

Preparation time 6 minutes
Cooking time 6–7 minutes

SERVES 4
8–12 shelled scallops
40g/1½ oz/3 tbsp butter
2.5cm/1in piece of fresh root ginger, finely chopped
1 bunch spring onions, diagonally sliced
60ml/4 tbsp white vermouth
250ml/8fl oz/1 cup crème fraîche
salt and ground black pepper
chopped fresh parsley, to garnish

1 Remove the tough muscle opposite the coral on each scallop. Separate the coral and cut the white part of the scallop in half horizontally.

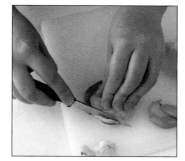

2 Melt the butter in a frying pan. Add the scallops, including the corals, and sauté for about 2 minutes until lightly browned. Take care not to overcook the scallops as this will toughen them. Lift out the scallops with a slotted spoon and transfer to a warmed serving dish. Keep hot.

3 Add the ginger and spring onions to the pan and stir-fry for 2 minutes. Pour in the vermouth and allow to bubble until it has almost evaporated. Stir in the crème fraîche and cook for a few minutes until thickened. Season.

4 Pour the sauce over the scallops, garnish and serve.

Thai Prawn Salad

This salad has the marvellous aromatic flavour of lemon grass.

Preparation time 17 minutes
Cooking time Nil

Serves 4
*250g/9oz cooked, peeled extra large
  tiger prawns
15ml/1 tbsp fish sauce
30ml/2 tbsp lime juice
7.5ml/1½ tsp soft light brown sugar
1 small red chilli, finely chopped
1 spring onion, finely chopped
1 small garlic clove, crushed
2.5cm/1in piece of fresh lemon grass,
  finely chopped
30ml/2 tbsp chopped fresh coriander
45ml/3 tbsp dry white wine
8–12 Little Gem lettuce leaves, to serve
fresh coriander sprigs, to garnish*

1 Place the tiger prawns in a bowl and add all the remaining ingredients except the lettuce. Stir well, cover and set aside for about 15 minutes, mixing and turning the prawns occasionally.

2 Arrange two or three of the lettuce leaves on each of four individual serving plates.

3 Spoon the prawn salad into the lettuce leaves. Garnish with fresh coriander and serve at once.

Cook's Tip
If you obtain raw prawns, cook them in boiling water until pink and use instead of the cooked prawns.

Cajun-Spiced Fish

Cajun food is becoming increasingly popular outside its native New Orleans, and no wonder, as dishes like this one cook quickly and taste absolutely superb.

Preparation time 2–3 minutes
Cooking time 10–13 minutes

Serves 4
*5ml/1 tsp dried thyme
5ml/1 tsp dried oregano
5ml/1 tsp ground black pepper
1.5ml/¼ tsp cayenne pepper
10ml/2 tsp paprika
2.5ml/½ tsp garlic salt
4 tail end pieces of cod fillet
  (about 175g/6oz each)
75g/3oz/⅓ cup butter
½ red pepper, seeded and sliced
½ green pepper, seeded and sliced
fresh thyme, to garnish
grilled tomatoes and sweet potato
  purée, to serve (optional)*

1 Place all the herbs and spices in a bowl and mix well. Lightly coat the fish in the spice mixture.

2 Heat 25g/1oz/2 tbsp of the butter in a frying pan, add the peppers and fry gently for 5 minutes. Remove the peppers and keep hot.

3 Add the remaining butter to the pan and heat until sizzling. Add the cod fillets; fry over a moderate heat for 3–4 minutes on each side, until browned and cooked.

4 Transfer the fish to a warmed serving dish, surround with the peppers and garnish with thyme. Serve the spiced fish with some grilled tomatoes and sweet potato purée, if you like.

Cook's Tip
This blend of herbs and spices can be used to flavour any fish steaks or fillets and could also be used to jazz up pan-fried prawns.

QUICK PITTA PIZZAS

Pitta breads make very good bases for quick thin and crispy pizzas, and they are easy to eat with your hands too. The perfect speedy snack.

Preparation time 5 minutes
Cooking time 8–10 minutes

Serves 4
4 pitta breads
200ml/7fl oz jar pasta sauce
225g/8oz mozzarella cheese, sliced
  or grated
dried oregano or thyme, to sprinkle
salt and ground black pepper
Extra toppings – choose from
1 small red onion, thinly sliced and
  lightly fried
75g/3oz/¾ cup button mushrooms,
  sliced and fried
200g/7oz can sweetcorn, drained
2 jalapeño chillies, sliced
black or green olives, stoned
  and sliced
capers, drained

1 Prepare two or three toppings of your choice for the pizzas.

2 Preheat the grill and lightly toast the pitta breads on both sides until golden.

COOK'S TIP
Teenagers love pitta pizzas, especially if they can assemble their own toppings. Strips of fried bacon and sliced pepperoni are great for non-vegetarians.

3 Spread pasta sauce on each pitta, right to the edge. This prevents the edges of the pitta from burning when they are returned to the grill.

4 Arrange cheese slices or grated cheese on top of each pitta and sprinkle with dried oregano or thyme. Add salt and pepper to taste.

5 Add the toppings of your choice and then grill the pizzas for about 5–8 minutes until they are golden brown and bubbling. Serve the pitta pizzas immediately.

FRENCH BREAD PIZZAS WITH ARTICHOKES

Crunchy French bread makes an ideal base for these quick pizzas.

Preparation time 4 minutes
Cooking time 14–16 minutes

SERVES 4

15ml/1 tbsp sunflower oil
1 onion, chopped
1 green pepper, seeded and chopped
200g/7oz can chopped tomatoes
15ml/1 tbsp tomato purée
½ French stick
400g/14oz can or jar artichoke
  hearts, drained
115g/4oz mozzarella cheese, sliced
15ml/1 tbsp poppy seeds
salt and ground black pepper

1   Heat the oil in a frying pan. Add the chopped onion and pepper and cook for 4 minutes until just softened.

2   Stir in the chopped tomatoes and the tomato purée. Cook for 4 minutes, stirring occasionally, then remove from the heat and add salt and pepper to taste.

3   Cut the piece of French stick in half lengthways. Cut each half in four to give eight pieces in all.

4   Spoon a little of the pepper and tomato mixture over each piece of bread. Preheat the grill.

5   Slice the artichoke hearts. Arrange them on top of the pepper and tomato mixture. Cover with the mozzarella slices and sprinkle with the poppy seeds.

6   Arrange the French bread pizzas on a rack over a grill pan and grill for 6–8 minutes until the cheese melts and is beginning to brown. Serve at once.

BRIOCHE WITH MIXED MUSHROOMS

Mushrooms, served on toasted brioche, make a delectable lunch.

Preparation time 3–4 minutes
Cooking time 15 minutes

SERVES 4
75g/3oz/ ¹/₃ cup butter
1 vegetable stock cube
450g/1lb/4 cups shiitake mushrooms,
  caps only, sliced
225g/8oz/2 cups button
  mushrooms, sliced
45ml/3 tbsp dry sherry
250ml/8fl oz/1 cup crème fraîche
10ml/2 tsp lemon juice
8 thick slices of brioche
salt and ground black pepper
fresh thyme, to garnish (optional)

1 Melt the butter in a large pan. Crumble in the stock cube and stir for about 30 seconds.

COOK'S TIP
If shiitake mushrooms are not available, substitute more button mushrooms.

2 Add the shiitake and button mushrooms to the pan and cook for 5 minutes over a moderate to high heat, stirring occasionally.

3 Stir in the dry sherry. Cook for 1 minute, then add the crème fraîche. Cook, stirring, over a gentle heat for 5 minutes. Stir in the lemon juice and add salt and pepper to taste. Preheat the grill.

4 Toast the brioche slices under the grill until just golden on both sides. Spoon the mushrooms on top, flash briefly under the grill, and serve. Fresh thyme can be used to garnish, if you like.

MIXED PEPPER PIPÉRADE

Preparation time 3–4 minutes
Cooking time 15 minutes

Serves 4
30ml/2 tbsp olive oil
1 onion, chopped
1 red pepper
1 green pepper
4 tomatoes, peeled and chopped
1 garlic clove, crushed
4 large eggs
ground black pepper
wholemeal toast, to serve

1 Heat the oil in a large frying pan and sauté the onion gently until it becomes softened.

2 Remove the seeds from the red and green peppers and slice them thinly. Stir the pepper slices into the onion and cook together gently for 5 minutes. Add the tomatoes and garlic, season with black pepper, and cook for a further 5 minutes or until the mixture has thickened slightly. In a small bowl, beat the eggs with 15ml/1 tbsp water.

3 Pour the egg mixture over the vegetables in the frying pan and cook for 2–3 minutes, stirring now and then, until the pipérade has thickened to the consistency of lightly scrambled eggs. Serve immediately with hot wholemeal toast.

COOK'S TIPS

Choose eggs that have been date-stamped for freshness. Do not stir the pipérade too much or the eggs may become rubbery.

BROCCOLI AND CAULIFLOWER GRATIN

Broccoli and cauliflower make an attractive combination, and this dish has a simple sauce based on yogurt.

Preparation time 3 minutes
Cooking time 11 minutes

SERVES 4

1 small cauliflower, about 250g/9oz
1 small head broccoli, about
 250g/9oz
150ml/ ¼ pint/ ⅔ cup natural yogurt
115g/4oz/1 cup grated Cheddar or
 Red Leicester cheese
5ml/1 tsp wholegrain mustard
30ml/2 tbsp wholemeal breadcrumbs
salt and ground black pepper

1 Break the cauliflower and broccoli into small florets, then cook in salted, boiling water for about 8 minutes, or until tender. Drain thoroughly, then transfer to a flameproof dish.

2 Mix the yogurt, cheese and mustard. Season with pepper and spoon over the cauliflower and broccoli. Preheat the grill.

3 Sprinkle the breadcrumbs over the top of the sauced vegetables and place under the hot grill until golden brown. Serve at once.

COOK'S TIP
When preparing the cauliflower and broccoli, discard the tougher part of the stalk, then break the florets into even-size pieces, so that they cook evenly. Any tender pieces of stalk on the broccoli can be peeled, thinly sliced and cooked with the florets.

CRACKED WHEAT AND FENNEL SALAD

Preparation time 18 minutes
Cooking time 2 minutes

SERVES 4

115g/4oz/ ³⁄₄ cup cracked wheat
115g/4oz green beans, chopped
1 large fennel bulb, finely chopped
1 small orange, rind grated
1 garlic clove, crushed
30–45ml/2–3 tbsp sunflower oil
15ml/1 tbsp white wine vinegar
salt and ground black pepper
chopped red or orange pepper,
*   to garnish*

1 Place the cracked wheat in a bowl and cover with boiling water. Leave for 10 minutes. Drain well and squeeze out any excess water. Tip into a bowl.

3 Add the garlic to the orange rind, then add the oil, wine vinegar and seasoning to taste, and mix thoroughly. Pour this dressing over the salad, mix well. If time permits, chill the salad for 1–2 hours.

2 Blanch the green beans in boiling water for 2 minutes. Drain. Stir into the drained wheat with the fennel. Peel and segment the orange and stir into the salad.

4 Serve the salad sprinkled with the red or orange pepper.

RUNNER BEANS WITH TOMATOES

Young runner beans should not have "strings" down the sides, but older ones will, and the strings should be removed before cooking.

Preparation time 2 minutes
Cooking time 13–18 minutes

SERVES 4
675g/1½lb runner beans, sliced
40g/1½oz/3 tbsp butter
4 ripe tomatoes, peeled and chopped
salt and ground black pepper
chopped fresh tarragon, to garnish

COOK'S TIP
French beans can be used instead of runner beans, but reduce the cooking time slightly.

|1| Add the beans to a saucepan of boiling water, return to the boil, then boil for 3 minutes. Drain well.

|2| Heat the butter in a saucepan and add the tomatoes, beans and seasoning. Cover the pan and simmer gently for 10–15 minutes, until the beans are tender.

|3| Tip the beans and tomatoes into a warm serving dish and sprinkle over the chopped tarragon. Serve hot as an accompaniment.

SPINACH AND BEETROOT SALAD

Preparation time 5 minutes
Cooking time 1 minute

SERVES 4–6
200g/7oz young spinach leaves
45ml/3 tbsp light olive oil
5ml/1 tsp caraway seeds
juice of 1 orange
5ml/1 tsp caster sugar
675g/1½lb cooked beetroot, diced
salt and ground black pepper
chopped fresh parsley, to garnish

|1| Arrange the spinach leaves in a shallow salad bowl.

|2| Heat the oil in a saucepan. Add the caraway seeds, orange juice and sugar. Shake over the heat to warm through.

|3| Add the beetroot and shake the pan to coat it with the dressing.

|4| Spoon the warm beetroot and dressing mixture over the spinach leaves and sprinkle with the chopped parsley. Serve at once either as an accompaniment or as a main course.

COOK'S TIP
Use freshly cooked beetroot, not those that have been steeped in vinegar.

VEGETABLE AND SATAY SALAD

To cook this tasty salad in the allotted time, you will need to cook the potatoes and the other vegetables simultaneously.

Preparation time 5 minutes
Cooking time 12–14 minutes

SERVES 4

450g/1lb baby new potatoes
1 small head cauliflower, broken into small florets
225g/8oz French beans, trimmed
400g/14oz can chick-peas, drained
115g/4oz/2 cups watercress sprigs
115g/4oz/2 cups beansprouts
8 spring onions, sliced
60ml/4 tbsp crunchy peanut butter
150ml/ ¼ pint/ ⅔ cup hot water
5ml/1 tsp chilli sauce
10ml/2 tsp soft brown sugar
5ml/1 tsp soy sauce
5ml/1 tsp lime juice

1 Put the potatoes into a pan and add water to just cover. Bring to the boil and cook for 10–12 minutes or until the potatoes are just tender when pierced with the point of a sharp knife. Drain and refresh under cold running water. Drain the potatoes again.

2 Meanwhile, bring another pan of salted water to the boil. Add the cauliflower and cook for about 5 minutes, then add the beans and cook for 5 minutes more. Drain both vegetables, refresh under cold water and drain again.

3 Put the cauliflower and beans into a large bowl and add the chick-peas. Halve the potatoes and add. Toss lightly. Mix the watercress, beansprouts and spring onions. Divide among four plates and pile the cooked vegetables on top.

4 Put the peanut butter into a bowl and stir in the water. Add the chilli sauce, brown sugar, soy sauce and lime juice. Whisk well then drizzle the dressing over the salad. Serve at once, with lime wedges, if you like.

COURGETTE PUFFS WITH MIXED LEAF SALAD

This unusual salad consists of deep-fried courgettes, flavoured with mint and served warm on a bed of salad leaves with a balsamic dressing.

Preparation time 5 minutes
Cooking time 6 minutes

SERVES 2–3
450g/1lb courgettes
75g/3oz/1¹/₂ cups fresh white breadcrumbs
1 egg
pinch of cayenne pepper
15ml/1 tbsp chopped fresh mint
oil for deep frying
15ml/1 tbsp balsamic vinegar
45ml/3 tbsp extra virgin olive oil
200g/7oz mixed salad leaves
salt and ground black pepper

1. Top and tail the courgettes. Coarsely grate them and put into a colander. Squeeze out the excess water, then put the courgettes into a bowl.

2. Add the white breadcrumbs, egg, cayenne pepper and chopped fresh mint, with salt and pepper to taste. Mix well, with a spoon or clean hands.

3. Shape the courgette and breadcrumb mixture into balls, about the size of walnuts.

4. Heat the oil for deep-frying to 180°C/350°F or until a cube of bread, when added to the oil, browns in 30–40 seconds. Deep-fry the courgette balls in batches for 2 minutes. Drain on kitchen paper.

5. Whisk the vinegar and oil together and season well.

6. Put the salad leaves in a bowl and pour over the dressing. Toss lightly to coat the leaves evenly. Add the courgette puffs and toss lightly together. Serve at once, while the courgette puffs are still crisp.

HERB OMELETTE WITH TOMATO SALAD

This is ideal as a snack or a light lunch – use flavourful, fresh plum tomatoes in season.

Preparation time 6 minutes
Cooking time 6 minutes

SERVES 4
4 eggs, beaten
30ml/2 tbsp chopped, mixed fresh herbs
knob of butter
45–60ml/3–4 tbsp olive oil
15ml/1 tbsp fresh orange juice
5ml/1 tsp red wine vinegar
5ml/1 tsp grainy mustard
2 large beef tomatoes, thinly sliced
salt and ground black pepper
fresh herb sprigs, to garnish

1 Beat the eggs, herbs and seasoning together. Heat the butter and a little of the oil in an omelette pan.

2 When the fats are just sizzling, pour in the egg mixture and leave to set for about 5 minutes until almost cooked through, stirring very occasionally with a fork.

3 Meanwhile, heat the rest of the oil in a small pan with the orange juice, vinegar and mustard, and add salt and pepper to taste.

4 Roll up the cooked omelette and cut neatly into 1cm/¹⁄₂in wide strips. Keep them rolled up and transfer immediately to warmed plates.

5 Arrange the sliced tomatoes on the plates with the omelette rolls and pour on the warm dressing. Garnish with herb sprigs and serve.

THREE-CHEESE CROÛTES

Preparation time 2–3 minutes
Cooking time 10–15 minutes

SERVES 2–4
4 thick slices of slightly stale bread
a little butter or mustard
75g/3oz Brie cheese
45ml/3 tbsp fromage frais
50g/2oz grated Parmesan or mature Cheddar cheese
1 small garlic clove, crushed
salt and ground black pepper
black olives, to garnish

COOK'S TIPS
If you have Brie that will not ripen fully, this is an excellent way of using it up. You'll need a knife and fork to eat this tasty starter. Instead of the simple black olive garnish, you could serve it with tangy whole-fruit cranberry sauce.

1 Preheat the oven to 200°C/ 400°F/Gas 6. Place the bread slices on a baking sheet and spread with either butter or mustard.

2 Cut the Brie into thin slices and arrange evenly on the bread.

3 Mix together the fromage frais, Parmesan or Cheddar, garlic, and seasoning to taste. Spread over the Brie and the bread, taking the mixture right to the corners.

4 Bake for 10–15 minutes, or until golden and bubbling. Serve immediately, garnished with black olives.

LEMON AND PARMESAN CAPELLINI WITH HERB BREAD

Cream is thickened with Parmesan and flavoured with lemon to make a superb sauce for pasta.

Preparation time 5 minutes
Cooking time 2–12 minutes

SERVES 2

½ Granary baguette
50g/2oz/ ¼ cup butter, softened
1 garlic clove, crushed
30ml/2 tbsp chopped fresh herbs
225g/8oz dried or fresh capellini
250ml/8fl oz/1 cup single cream
75g/3oz Parmesan cheese, grated
finely grated rind of 1 lemon
salt and ground black pepper

1 Preheat the oven to 200°C/ 400°F/Gas 6. Cut the baguette into thick slices.

2 Put the butter in a bowl and beat with the garlic and herbs. Spread thickly over each slice of Granary bread.

3 Reassemble the baguette. The garlic herb butter will help to hold the slices together. Wrap in foil, support on a baking sheet and bake for 10 minutes.

4 Meanwhile, bring a large pan of water to the boil and cook the pasta until just tender. Dried pasta will take 10–12 minutes; fresh pasta will be ready in 2–3 minutes.

5 Pour the cream into another pan and bring to the boil. Stir in the Parmesan and lemon rind. The sauce should thicken in 30 seconds or so.

6 Drain the pasta, return it to the pan and toss with the sauce. Season to taste and sprinkle with a little chopped fresh parsley and more grated lemon rind, if you like. Serve with the hot herb bread.

TAGLIATELLE WITH TOMATOES AND BLACK OLIVES

Sun-dried tomatoes add pungency to this dish, while the grilled fresh tomatoes give it a bit of bite.

Preparation time 5 minutes
Cooking time 10–12 minutes

SERVES 4

45ml/3 tbsp olive oil
1 garlic clove, crushed
1 small onion, chopped
60ml/4 tbsp dry white wine
6 sun-dried tomatoes, chopped
30ml/2 tbsp chopped fresh parsley
50g/2oz/ ¹/₂ cup stoned black
  olives, halved
450g/1lb fresh tagliatelle
4 tomatoes, halved
Parmesan cheese, to serve
salt and ground black pepper

1. Heat 30ml/2 tbsp of the oil in a pan. Add the garlic and onion and cook for 2–3 minutes, stirring occasionally. Add the wine, sun-dried tomatoes and the parsley. Cook for 2 minutes. Stir in the black olives, lower the heat and leave the sauce over a low heat.

COOK'S TIP
It is essential to buy Parmesan in a piece for this dish. Find a good source – fresh Parmesan should not be unacceptably hard – and shave or grate it yourself. The flavour will be much more intense than that of the ready-grated product.

2. Preheat the grill. Bring a large pan of salted water to the boil. Add the fresh tagliatelle and cook for 2–3 minutes.

3. Put the tomatoes on a baking sheet and brush with the remaining oil. Grill for 3–4 minutes.

4. When the pasta rises to the surface of the boiling water, it is ready. Drain it thoroughly, return it to the pan and toss with the sauce. Pile into a bowl and add the grilled tomatoes. Grind black pepper over the top and add Parmesan shavings.

PASTA WITH BROCCOLI AND ARTICHOKES

Preparation time 5 minutes
Cooking time 13 minutes

SERVES 4
105ml/7 tbsp olive oil
1 red pepper, quartered, seeded, and
   thinly sliced
1 onion, halved and thinly sliced
5ml/1 tsp dried thyme
45ml/3 tbsp sherry vinegar
450g/1lb fresh or dried pasta shapes,
   such as penne or fusilli
2 x 175g/6oz jars marinated
   artichoke hearts, drained and
   thinly sliced
150g/5oz cooked broccoli, chopped
20–25 black olives, pitted
   and chopped
30ml/2 tbsp chopped fresh parsley
salt and ground black pepper

1 Heat 30ml/2 tbsp of the oil in a non-stick frying pan. Add the red pepper and onion and cook over a low heat for 8–10 minutes, or until the vegetables are just soft, stirring occasionally.

2 Stir in the thyme and sherry vinegar. Cook for 30 seconds more, stirring, then set aside.

3 Meanwhile, cook the pasta in a large pan of boiling salted water until just tender (10–12 minutes for dried; 2–3 minutes for fresh). Drain, then transfer to a serving large bowl. Add 30ml/2 tbsp of the oil and toss well to coat.

4 Add the artichokes, broccoli, olives, parsley, onion mixture and remaining oil to the pasta. Season with salt and pepper. Toss to blend. Leave to stand for 5 minutes before serving, longer if time permits.

PASTA WITH SPRING VEGETABLES

Preparation and
cooking time 20 minutes

SERVES 4

115g/4oz/1 cup broccoli florets
115g/4oz baby leeks
225g/8oz asparagus, trimmed
1 small fennel bulb
115g/4oz/2 cups fresh or frozen peas
40g/1½ oz/3 tbsp butter
1 shallot, chopped
45ml/3 tbsp chopped fresh mixed herbs,
*   such as parsley, thyme and sage*
300ml/½ pint/1¼ cups double cream
350g/12oz dried penne pasta
salt and ground black pepper
freshly grated Parmesan cheese,
*   to serve*

1 Divide the broccoli florets into tiny sprigs. Cut the leeks and asparagus diagonally into 5cm/2in lengths. Trim the fennel bulb and cut into wedges.

2 Cook the vegetables in boiling salted water until just tender. Remove with a slotted spoon and keep hot.

3 Melt the butter in a separate pan, add the chopped shallot and cook, stirring occasionally, until softened, but not browned. Stir in the herbs and cream and cook for a few minutes, until slightly thickened.

4 Meanwhile, cook the pasta in boiling salted water until just tender. Drain well and add to the sauce with the vegetables. Toss gently and season with black pepper.

5 Serve the pasta at once with a generous sprinkling of freshly grated Parmesan.

RED FRIED RICE

This vibrant rice dish owes its appeal as much to the bright colours of red onion, red pepper and cherry tomatoes as it does to their distinctive flavours.

Preparation time 3–4 minutes
Cooking time 13–15 minutes

SERVES 2

225g/8oz/1 cup basmati rice
30ml/2 tbsp groundnut oil
1 large red onion, chopped
1 red pepper, seeded and chopped
350g/12oz cherry tomatoes, halved
4 eggs, beaten
salt and ground black pepper

1 Wash the rice several times in a bowl of cold water. Drain well. Bring a large pan of water to the boil, add the rice and cook for 10–12 minutes.

2 Meanwhile, heat the oil in a wok until very hot. Add the onion and red pepper and stir-fry for 2–3 minutes. Add the cherry tomatoes and stir-fry for a further 2 minutes.

3 Pour in the beaten eggs all at once. Cook for 30 seconds without stirring, then stir to break up the egg as it sets.

4 Drain the cooked rice thoroughly, add to the wok and toss it over the heat with the egg and vegetable mixture for 3 minutes. Season to taste.

KEDGEREE WITH FRENCH BEANS AND MUSHROOMS

Crunchy, cooked French beans and brown cap mushrooms are the star ingredients in this vegetarian version of an old favourite.

Preparation time 3–4 minutes
Cooking time 16 minutes

SERVES 2–3
115g/4oz/scant ¾ cup basmati rice
3 eggs
175g/6oz French beans, trimmed
50g/2oz/ ¼ cup butter
1 onion, finely chopped
225g/8oz/2 cups brown cap
  mushrooms, quartered
30ml/2 tbsp single cream
15ml/1 tbsp chopped fresh parsley
salt and ground black pepper

1 Wash the rice several times in a bowl of cold water. Drain thoroughly. Bring a pan of water to the boil, add the rice and cook for 10–12 minutes until the grains are just tender.

2 Meanwhile, half fill a second pan with water, add the eggs and bring to the boil. Lower the heat and simmer for 8 minutes. Drain the eggs, cool them under cold water, then remove the shells.

3 Bring another pan of water to the boil and cook the French beans for 5 minutes. Drain, refresh under cold running water, then drain again.

4 Melt the butter in a large frying pan. Add the onion and mushrooms. Cook for 2–3 minutes over a moderate heat.

VARIATION
Leave out the beans and cook two sliced celery sticks with the onion and mushrooms. Garnish with toasted almonds.

5 Drain the rice well and add it to the onion mixture with the beans. Stir lightly. Cook for about 2 minutes. Cut the hard-boiled eggs in wedges and add them to the pan.

6 Stir in the cream and parsley, taking care not to break up the eggs. Reheat the kedgeree, but do not allow it to boil. Serve at once.

Red Fruit Filo Baskets

Filo pastry is light as air and makes a very elegant dessert.

Preparation time 8 minutes
Cooking time 6–8 minutes

SERVES 6

3 sheets filo pastry (about 90g/3½oz)
15ml/1 tbsp sunflower oil
175g/6oz/1½ cups soft fruits, such as
*   redcurrants, strawberries*
*   and raspberries*
250ml/8fl oz/1 cup Greek yogurt
5ml/1 tsp icing sugar

1 Preheat the oven to 200°C/400°F/Gas 6. Cut the sheets of filo pastry into 18 squares with sides about 10cm/4in long. Cover the filo with clear film to stop it from drying out.

2 Brush each filo square very thinly with oil, and then arrange the squares overlapping in six small patty tins, layering them in threes. Bake for 6–8 minutes, until crisp and golden. Lift the baskets out carefully and leave them to cool for 5–10 minutes on a wire rack.

3 Reserve a few sprigs of redcurrants on their stems for decoration and string the rest. Stir into the yogurt with the strawberries and raspberries.

4 Spoon the yogurt mixture into the filo baskets. Decorate them with the reserved sprigs of redcurrants and sprinkle them with icing sugar to serve.

VARIATIONS
Other soft fruits can be used instead of redcurrants, strawberries and raspberries. Try blueberries or blackberries for a change, or use sliced bananas, nectarines, peaches or kiwi fruit.

APPLE SOUFFLÉ OMELETTE

Apples sautéed until they are soft and slightly caramelized make a delicious autumn filling.

Preparation time 3–4 minutes
Cooking time 8 minutes

SERVES 2

4 eggs, separated
30ml/2 tbsp single cream
15ml/1 tbsp caster sugar
15g/ 1/2 oz/1 tbsp butter
icing sugar, for dredging
For the filling
1 eating apple, peeled, cored
  and sliced
25g/1oz/2 tbsp butter
30ml/2 tbsp soft light brown sugar
45ml/3 tbsp single cream

1   To make the filling, sauté the apple slices in the butter and sugar until just tender. Stir in the cream and keep warm.

2   Beat the egg yolks with the cream and sugar. Whisk the egg whites until stiff, then fold into the yolk mixture. Preheat the grill.

3   Melt the butter in a large heavy-based frying pan, pour in the soufflé mixture and spread evenly. Cook until golden underneath, then brown the top under the grill.

4   Slide the omelette on to a plate, add the apple mixture, then fold over. Sift the icing sugar over thickly, then brand with a hot metal skewer. Serve immediately.

PINEAPPLE FLAMBÉ

Flambéing means adding alcohol and then burning it off so the flavour is not too overpowering.

Preparation time 5 minutes
Cooking time 1–2 minutes

SERVES 4
1 large, ripe pineapple
40g/1½oz/3 tbsp unsalted butter
40g/1½oz/3 tbsp soft light brown sugar
60ml/4 tbsp fresh orange juice
30ml/2 tbsp brandy
25g/1oz/2 tbsp slivered almonds, toasted

1 Cut away the top and base of the pineapple. Then cut down the sides, removing all the dark "eyes", but leaving the pineapple in a good shape.

2 Cut the pineapple into thin slices and, with an apple corer, remove the hard central core.

3 In a large frying pan melt the butter with the sugar and orange juice. Add the pineapple slices and cook for about a minute, turning the slices once.

4 Add the brandy and light with a match immediately. Let the flames die down and then sprinkle with the almonds and serve with ice cream or thick yogurt.

WARM PEARS IN CIDER

Preparation and
cooking time 20 minutes

SERVES 4
1 lemon
50g/2oz/¼ cup caster sugar
a little grated nutmeg
250ml/8fl oz/1 cup sweet cider
4 firm, ripe pears

1 Carefully remove the rind from the lemon with a potato peeler leaving any white pith behind.

2 Squeeze the juice from the lemon into a saucepan, add the rind, sugar, nutmeg and cider and heat through to dissolve the sugar.

3 Carefully peel the pears, leaving the stalks on if possible, and place them in the pan of sweetened, spiced cider. Poach the pears over a medium heat for 10–15 minutes until almost tender, turning them frequently.

4 Transfer the pears to individual serving dishes using a slotted spoon. Simmer the liquid over a high heat until it reduces slightly and becomes syrupy.

5 Pour the warm syrup over the pears, and serve at once with freshly made custard, whipped cream or ice cream.

COOK'S TIP
To get pears of just the right firmness, you may have to buy them slightly under-ripe and then wait a day or more. Soft pears are no good at all for this dish.

COOL GREEN FRUIT SALAD

A sophisticated, simple fruit salad for any time of year.

Preparation time 20 minutes
Cooking time 30 seconds

SERVES 6

3 Ogen or Galia melons
115g/4oz/1 cup green seedless grapes
2 kiwi fruit
1 star fruit
1 green-skinned apple
1 lime
175ml/6fl oz/ ¾ cup sparkling white grape juice

1 Cut the melons in half and scoop out the seeds. Keeping the shells intact, scoop out the flesh with a melon baller, or scoop it out with a spoon and cut into bite-size cubes. Reserve the melon shells.

2 Remove any stems from the grapes, and, if they are large, cut them in half. Peel and chop the kiwi fruit. Thinly slice the star fruit. Core and thinly slice the apple and place the slices in a bowl, with the melon, grapes, kiwi fruit and star fruit. Mix gently.

3 Thinly pare the rind from the lime and cut it in fine strips. Blanch the strips in boiling water for 30 seconds, and then drain them and rinse them in cold water. Squeeze the juice from the lime and toss it into the fruit.

4 Spoon the prepared fruit into the reserved melon shells. Chill the shells if you have time, or serve at once, spooning the sparkling grape juice over the fruit and scattering it with the lime rind.

COOK'S TIP
If you're serving this dessert on a hot summer day, serve the filled melon shells nestling on a platter of crushed ice to keep them beautifully cool.

PRUNE AND ORANGE POTS

A simple, storecupboard dessert, made in minutes. It can be served straight away, but is best chilled for about half an hour before serving.

Preparation time 4 minutes
Cooking time 7 minutes

SERVES 4

225g/8oz/1 cup ready-to-eat prunes
150ml/ ¼ pint/ ⅔ cup fresh
orange juice
250ml/8fl oz/1 cup natural yogurt
thin shreds of orange rind,
to decorate

VARIATIONS

This dessert can also be made with other ready-to-eat dried fruit, such as apricots or peaches. For a special occasion, add a dash of brandy or Cointreau with the yogurt.

1 Remove the stones from the prunes and roughly chop them. Place them in a pan and pour in the orange juice.

2 Bring the juice to the boil, stirring. Reduce the heat, cover and leave to simmer for 5 minutes, until the prunes are tender and the liquid is reduced by half.

3 Remove from the heat, allow to cool slightly and then beat well with a wooden spoon, until the fruit breaks down to a rough purée.

4 Transfer the mixture to a bowl. Stir in the yogurt, swirling the yogurt and fruit purée together lightly with a spoon, to give an attractive marbled effect.

5 Spoon the mixture into four stemmed glasses or individual dishes. Smooth the tops, but don't lose the swirled effect.

6 Blanch the shreds of orange rind in boiling water, drain and use a few shreds to decorate each dessert. Serve at once or chill if time permits.

Orange Yogurt Brûlées

A luxurious treat, but one that is much lower in fat than the classic brûlées, which are made with cream, eggs and large amounts of sugar.

Preparation time 6–8 minutes
Cooking time 3–4 minutes

SERVES 4
2 oranges
150ml/ ¹/₄ pint/ ²/₃ cup Greek yogurt
60ml/4 tbsp crème fraîche
45ml/3 tbsp golden
  caster sugar
30ml/2 tbsp light muscovado sugar

1 With a sharp knife, cut away all the peel and white pith from the oranges and chop the fruit. Or, if there's time, segment the oranges, removing all the membrane.

2 Place the fruit in the bottom of four individual flameproof dishes. Mix together the yogurt and crème fraîche and spoon the mixture over the oranges. Preheat the grill.

3 Mix together the two sugars and sprinkle them thickly and evenly over the tops of the dishes.

4 Place the dishes under the grill, close to the heat, for 3–4 minutes or until the sugar melts and turns a rich golden brown. Serve warm or cold.

COOK'S TIP
For a lighter version, simply use 250ml/8fl oz/1 cup low-fat natural yogurt instead of the mixture of Greek yogurt and crème fraîche.

GRILLED NECTARINES WITH RICOTTA AND SPICE

This easy dessert is good at any time of year — use canned peach halves if fresh nectarines are not available.

Preparation time 3 minutes
Cooking time 6–8 minutes

SERVES 4
4 ripe nectarines
115g/4oz/ ½ cup ricotta cheese or
fromage frais
15ml/1 tbsp light muscovado sugar
2.5ml/ ½ tsp ground star anise

1 Cut the nectarines in half and remove the stones.

2 Arrange the nectarines, cut-side up, in a wide flameproof dish or on a baking sheet.

COOK'S TIP
Star anise has a warm, rich flavour – if you can't get it, try ground cloves or ground mixed spice instead.

3 Put the ricotta or fromage frais in a bowl and stir in the sugar. Using a teaspoon, spoon the mixture into the hollow of each nectarine half. Preheat the grill.

4 Sprinkle with the star anise. Place under the grill and bake for 6–8 minutes, or until the nectarines are hot and bubbling. Serve warm.

30 MINUTE RECIPES

If you've cooked your way right through this book, having half an hour at your disposal will seem like unimaginable luxury. The recipes in this section are so deliciously imaginative, however, that you could easily waste ten minutes deciding what to try. Shall it be Turkey Rolls with Gazpacho Sauce, Duck Breasts with Calvados or those scrumptious Sole Goujons with Lime Mayonnaise? Whatever you choose, leave room for a speedy sweet such as Nectarine Puff Pastry Tarts or Amaretto Soufflé.

WATERCRESS AND ORANGE SOUP

This refreshing and healthy soup is great hot or cold.

Preparation time 5 minutes
Cooking time 20 minutes

SERVES 4

15ml/1 tbsp olive oil
1 large onion, chopped
2 bunches or bags of watercress
grated rind and juice of 1 orange
600ml/1 pint/2½ cups vegetable
  stock
150ml/ ¼ pint/ ⅔ cup single cream
10ml/2 tsp cornflour
salt and ground black pepper
a little thick cream, to garnish
4 orange wedges, to serve

1 Heat the oil in a large pan and fry the onion until softened. Trim any large, thick stalks from the watercress, then add to the pan of onion without chopping. Cover and cook for about 5 minutes.

2 Add the grated orange rind and juice, then pour in the vegetable stock. Bring to the boil, cover, lower the heat and simmer for about 10 minutes. Purée the soup in a blender or food processor. Return it to the pan. Add the cream blended with the cornflour, and season to taste with salt and pepper.

3 Bring the soup gently back to the boil, stirring until just slightly thickened. Check the seasoning and serve the soup topped with a swirl of cream. Offer a wedge of orange to squeeze in at the last moment.

MUSHROOM AND HERB SOUP

Although you can make mushroom soup with a nice smooth texture, it is more time consuming and you waste a lot of mushrooms — so enjoy the slightly nutty consistency instead!

Preparation time 5 minutes
Cooking time 20 minutes

SERVES 4

50g/2oz rindless smoked streaky
   bacon rashers
1 white onion, chopped
15ml/1 tbsp sunflower oil
350g/12oz/3 cups flat cap field
   mushrooms or a mixture of wild
   and brown mushrooms
600ml/1 pint/2¹/₂ cups beef stock
30ml/2 tbsp sweet sherry
30ml/2 tbsp chopped, mixed fresh
   herbs, or 10ml/2 tsp dried herbs
salt and ground black pepper
60ml/4 tbsp thick Greek yogurt or
   crème fraîche and a few sprigs of
   marjoram or sage, to garnish

4 Return to the pan and heat
   through. Serve with a dollop of
yogurt or crème fraîche and a herb
sprig in each bowl.

1 Roughly chop the bacon and
   place in a large saucepan. Cook
gently until all the fat comes out of
the bacon.

2 Add the onion, with the oil, and
   cook until softened. Wipe the
mushrooms clean, chop them roughly
and add to the pan. Cover and cook
over a low heat until they have
softened completely and yielded
their liquid.

3 Add the stock, sherry, herbs
   and seasoning, cover and
simmer for 10–12 minutes. Blend or
process the soup until fairly smooth,
but with some texture.

CARROT AND CORIANDER SOUP

Carrot soup is best made with young carrots when they are at their sweetest and tastiest. With older carrots you will have to use more to get the full flavour.

Preparation time 5 minutes
Cooking time 20–25 minutes

SERVES 5–6
1 onion, chopped
15ml/1 tbsp sunflower oil
675g/1½ lb carrots, chopped
900ml/1½ pint/3¾ cups chicken stock
few sprigs of fresh coriander, or
  5ml/1 tsp dried coriander
5ml/1 tsp lemon rind
30ml/2 tbsp lemon juice
salt and ground black pepper
chopped fresh parsley or coriander,
  to garnish

1 Soften the onion in the oil in a large pan. Add the chopped carrots, the stock, coriander, lemon rind and juice. Season to taste.

2 Bring to the boil, cover and cook for 15–20 minutes. When the carrots are really tender, purée the soup in a blender or food processor, return it to the pan, then check the seasoning.

3 Heat through again and sprinkle with chopped parsley or coriander before serving.

PRAWN AND SWEETCORN CHOWDER

This quick and easy soup is perfect for informal entertaining.

Preparation time 3 minutes
Cooking time 23 minutes

SERVES 4
15g/½oz/1 tbsp butter
1 onion, chopped
300g/11oz can sweetcorn
30ml/2 tbsp lemon juice
300ml/½ pint/1¼ cups fish stock
115g/4oz/1 cup cooked, peeled
  prawns
300ml/½ pint/1¼ cups milk
15–30ml/1–2 tbsp single cream
salt and ground black pepper
4 large prawns in their shells and a
  few parsley or dill sprigs, to garnish

1 Heat the butter in a pan and cook the onion until translucent. Add half the sweetcorn and all the can liquid, the lemon juice, stock and half the prawns.

2 Cover and simmer the soup for about 15 minutes, then purée in a food processor or blender.

3 Return the soup to the pan and add the milk. Chop the rest of the prawns, and add them with the sweetcorn and cream. Season to taste with salt and pepper, then cook gently for 5 minutes, or until reduced sufficiently.

4 Ladle the carrot and coriander soup into warmed bowls. Serve each portion garnished with a whole prawn and a herb sprig. Serve with warm ciabatta bread, if you like.

Thai Chicken Soup

Preparation time 4 minutes
Cooking time 23–24 minutes

SERVES 4

15ml/1 tbsp vegetable oil
1 garlic clove, finely chopped
2 skinless, boneless chicken breasts,
    175g/6oz each, chopped
2.5ml/ ½ tsp ground turmeric
1.5ml/ ¼ tsp hot chilli powder
75g/3oz/ ½ cup creamed coconut
900ml/1½ pints/3¼ cups hot chicken
    stock
30ml/2 tbsp lemon or lime juice
30ml/2 tbsp crunchy peanut butter
50g/2oz/1 cup thread egg noodles,
    broken into small pieces
15ml/1 tbsp spring onions, chopped
15ml/1 tbsp chopped fresh coriander
salt and ground black pepper
desiccated coconut and finely
    chopped red chilli, to garnish

1 Heat the oil in a large pan and fry the garlic for 1 minute until lightly golden. Add the chicken and spices. Stir-fry for 3–4 minutes.

2 Crumble the creamed coconut into the hot chicken stock and stir until dissolved. Pour on to the chicken and add the lemon juice, peanut butter and egg noodles.

3 Cover the pan and simmer for 15 minutes. Add the spring onions and fresh coriander, season well and cook for a further 5 minutes.

4 Meanwhile, heat the coconut and chilli in a small frying pan for 2–3 minutes, stirring frequently, until the coconut is lightly browned.

5 Serve the soup sprinkled with the dry-fried coconut and chilli.

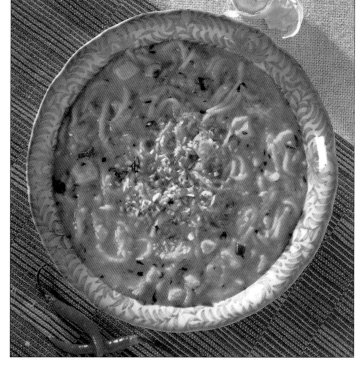

PASTA AND BEAN SOUP

*Serve this hearty main-meal soup
with tasty, pesto-topped French
bread croûtons.*

**Preparation time 8 minutes
Cooking time 18 minutes**

Serves 4

*15ml/1 tbsp oil
1 onion, chopped
2 celery sticks, thinly sliced
2–3 garlic cloves, crushed
2 leeks, thinly sliced
425g/15oz can red kidney or
    mixed beans
600ml/1 pint/2½ cups vegetable stock
400g/14oz can or jar of pimientos
45–60ml/3–4 tbsp tomato purée
115g/4oz/1 cup pasta shapes
4 pieces French bread
15ml/1 tbsp pesto sauce
115g/4oz/²⁄₃ cup baby corn, halved
50g/2oz/½ cup each broccoli and
    cauliflower florets
few drops of Tabasco sauce, to taste
salt and ground black pepper*

☐1 Preheat the oven to 200°C/
400°F/Gas 6. Heat the oil in a
large pan and fry the onion, celery,
garlic and leeks over a medium heat
for 2 minutes, stirring occasionally.

☐2 Drain the kidney beans or
mixed beans and add them to
the pan with the vegetable stock.
Bring to the boil, then lower the heat.
Cover the pan and simmer for about
10 minutes.

☐3 Meanwhile, purée all the
pimientos with a little of their
liquid and add to the pan. Stir in the
tomato purée and pasta shapes and
cook for 15 minutes.

☐4 Meanwhile, make the pesto
croûtons. Spread the French
bread with the pesto sauce and bake
for about 10 minutes, or until crisp.

☐5 When the pasta is just cooked,
add the baby corn, broccoli and
cauliflower florets to the soup and
stir in Tabasco sauce and salt and
pepper to taste. Heat through for
2–3 minutes and serve at once with
the pesto croûtons.

Creamy Cauliflower and Walnut Soup

Even though there's no cream added to this soup, the cauliflower gives it a delicious, rich, creamy texture.

Preparation time 2–3 minutes
Cooking time 20 minutes

SERVES 4
1 cauliflower
1 onion, coarsely chopped
450ml/ ³/₄ pint/scant 2 cups chicken
  or vegetable stock
450ml/ ³/₄ pint/scant 2 cups milk
45ml/3 tbsp walnut pieces
salt and ground black pepper
paprika and chopped walnuts,
  to garnish

1. Trim the cauliflower of outer leaves and break into small florets. Place the cauliflower, onion, and stock in a large saucepan. Bring to the boil, cover, lower the heat and simmer for 15 minutes.

2. Pour the mixture into a food processor or blender in batches if necessary, then add the milk and walnuts. Purée until smooth.

VARIATION
Use ground almonds in place of walnuts.

3. Return the soup to the clean pan, season to taste, then bring it to the boil. Serve in heated bowls, sprinkled with a little paprika and chopped walnuts.

Curried Carrot and Apple Soup

Preparation time 5 minutes
Cooking time 20 minutes

SERVES 4
10ml/2 tsp sunflower oil
15ml/1 tbsp mild curry powder
  or paste
500g/1¹/₄ lb carrots, chopped
1 large onion, chopped
1 cooking apple, chopped
750ml/1¹/₄ pints/3 cups chicken or
  vegetable stock
salt and ground black pepper
natural yogurt and carrot curls,
  to garnish

COOK'S TIP
Choose an acidic apple, such as a Bramley, that will soften and fluff up as it cooks. Peel it if you like, but this is not essential. Chop it into fairly small pieces before adding it to the pan.

1. Heat the oil and gently fry the curry powder for 2–3 minutes.

2. Add the carrots, onion and apple. Stir then cover the pan.

3. Cook over very low heat for about 15 minutes, shaking the pan occasionally until softened. Spoon the mixture into a food processor or blender, then add half the stock and process until smooth.

4. Return to the pan and pour in the remaining stock. Bring the soup to the boil, stirring and adjust the seasoning before serving in heated bowls. Garnish with swirled yogurt and carrot curls.

CHINESE GARLIC MUSHROOMS

Tofu is high in protein and very low in fat, so it is a very useful food to keep handy. It makes a very tasty stuffing for mushrooms.

Preparation time 5 minutes
Cooking time 15–20 minutes

SERVES 4

8 large open cup mushrooms
3 spring onions, sliced
1 garlic clove, crushed
30ml/2 tbsp oyster sauce
285g/10½ oz packet marinated tofu,
   cut into small dice
200g/7oz can sweetcorn, drained
10ml/2 tsp sesame oil
salt and ground black pepper

1 Preheat the oven to 200°C/ 400°F/Gas 6. Finely chop the mushroom stalks; mix with the spring onions, garlic and oyster sauce.

2 Stir in the diced marinated tofu and sweetcorn, season well with salt and pepper, then spoon the filling into the mushrooms.

3 Brush the edges of the mushrooms with the sesame oil. Arrange the stuffed mushrooms in a baking dish and bake for about 15–20 minutes, until the mushrooms are just tender. Serve at once.

COOK'S TIP
If you prefer, omit the oyster sauce and use light soy sauce instead.

MUSSELS WITH CREAM AND PARSLEY

Preparation time 10–12 minutes
Cooking time 10 minutes

SERVES 2

675g/1¹/₂lb mussels in the shell
¹/₂ fennel bulb, finely chopped
1 shallot, finely chopped
45ml/3 tbsp dry white wine
45ml/3 tbsp single cream
30ml/2 tbsp chopped fresh parsley

[1] Scrub the mussels under cold running water. Tear away the beards and discard any that remain open when tapped. Rinse once more.

[2] Place the mussels in a large wide pan with a lid. Sprinkle them with the fennel, shallot and wine. Cover and place over a medium-high heat, shaking the pan occasionally. Steam for 3–5 minutes, until the mussels open.

[3] Lift out the mussels with a slotted spoon and remove the top shells. Discard any that did not open. Arrange the mussels, on their bottom shells, in a shallow serving dish. Cover and keep hot.

[4] Place a double layer of dampened muslin or a clean dish towel in a sieve set over a bowl. Strain the mussel cooking liquid through this into a clean saucepan and bring to the boil.

[5] Add the cream, stir well and boil for 3 minutes to reduce slightly, then stir in the parsley. Spoon the sauce over the mussels. Sprinkle with pepper, if you like. Serve the mussels immediately.

BEETROOT AND HERRING SALAD

This colourful salad uses fresh beetroot — too often underrated.

Preparation time 5–6 minutes
Cooking time Nil

SERVES 4–6
350g/12oz cooked beetroot, skinned and thickly sliced
30ml/2 tbsp vinaigrette dressing
4 rollmop herrings, drained
350g/12oz cooked waxy salad potatoes, thickly sliced
½ small red onion, thinly sliced and separated into rings
150ml/¼ pint/⅔ cup soured cream
30ml/2 tbsp snipped fresh chives
dark rye bread, to serve

1 Mix the sliced cooked beetroot with the dressing. Arrange the herrings on individual plates with the beetroot, potatoes and onion.

2 Add a generous spoonful of the soured cream to each serving and sprinkle with snipped chives. Serve with dark rye bread.

GARLIC PRAWNS IN FILO TARTLETS

Tartlets made with crisp layers of filo pastry and filled with garlic prawns make a tempting starter.

Preparation time 8 minutes
Cooking time 10–15 minutes

SERVES 4
50g/2oz/¼ cup butter, melted
2–3 large sheets filo pastry
For the filling
115g/4oz/½ cup butter
2–3 garlic cloves, crushed
1 red chilli, seeded and chopped
350g/12oz cooked, peeled king prawns
30ml/2 tbsp chopped fresh parsley or snipped fresh chives
salt and ground black pepper

1 Preheat the oven to 200°C/ 400°F/Gas 6. Brush four individual 7.5cm/3in flan tins with melted butter.

2 Cut the filo pastry into twelve 10cm/4in squares and brush with the melted butter.

3 Place three filo pastry squares inside each flan tin, overlapping them at slight angles and carefully frilling the edges and points while forming a good hollow in each centre. Bake for 10–15 minutes, until crisp and golden brown.

4 Meanwhile, make the filling. Melt the butter in a large frying pan, and fry the garlic, chilli and prawns for 1–2 minutes to warm through. Stir in the parsley or chives and season well.

5 Remove the tartlets from the tins and place on individual plates. Spoon in the prawn filling and serve.

COOK'S TIP
Use fresh filo pastry, rather than frozen, then freeze any leftover sheets.

BAKED EGGS WITH CREAMY LEEKS

The French have traditionally enjoyed eggs prepared in many different ways. Vary this simple yet elegant dish by using other vegetables, such as puréed spinach, or ratatouille, as a base.

Preparation time 2 minutes
Cooking time 17–20 minutes

SERVES 4

15g/ ¹/₂oz/1 tbsp butter, plus extra for greasing
225g/8oz small leeks, thinly sliced (about 2 cups)
75–90ml/5–6 tbsp whipping cream
freshly grated nutmeg
4 eggs
salt and ground black pepper

1 Preheat the oven to 190°C/ 375°F/Gas 5. Generously butter the base and sides of four ramekins or individual soufflé dishes. Set them aside while you cook the leeks.

2 Melt the butter in a small frying pan and cook the leeks over a medium heat, stirring frequently, until softened but not browned.

3 Add 45ml/3 tbsp of the cream and cook gently for 5 minutes until the leeks are very soft and the cream has thickened a little. Season with salt, pepper and nutmeg.

4 Arrange the ramekins in a small roasting tin and divide the leeks among them. Break an egg into each. Spoon 5–10ml/1–2 tsp of the remaining cream over each egg and season lightly.

5 Pour boiling water into the roasting tin to come halfway up the sides of the ramekins or soufflé dishes. Bake for 10 minutes, until the whites are set and the yolks are still soft, or a little longer if you prefer your eggs a little firmer. Serve at once.

CHEESE-STUFFED PEARS

These pears, with their scrumptious creamy topping, make a sublime dish when served with a simple salad.

Preparation time 5 minutes
Cooking time 23 minutes

SERVES 4

50g/2oz/ ¼ cup ricotta cheese
50g/2oz/ ¼ cup dolcelatte cheese
15ml/1 tbsp clear honey
½ celery stick, finely sliced
3 green olives, stoned and
  roughly chopped
4 dates, stoned and cut into strips
pinch of paprika
4 ripe pears
150ml/ ¼ pint/ ⅔ cup apple juice
green salad, to serve

1 Preheat the oven to 200°C/
   400°F/Gas 6. Place the ricotta in a bowl and crumble in the dolcelatte. Add the rest of the ingredients except for the pears and apple juice and mix well.

2 Halve the pears lengthways and use a melon baller to remove the cores. Place in an ovenproof dish and divide the filling equally between them, piling it up.

3 Pour the apple juice into the dish carefully, taking care not to disturb the filled pears. Cover the dish with foil. Bake for 20 minutes or until the pears are tender when pierced with a skewer or the point of a sharp knife. Preheat the grill. Remove the foil from the dish.

4 Place the dish under the hot grill for about 3 minutes. Serve immediately with green salad.

COOK'S TIP
Choose ripe pears in season such as Conference, William or Comice.

TURKEY ROLLS WITH GAZPACHO SAUCE

Cook these wonderful turkey rolls, with their spicy sausage centres, on the barbecue or under the grill. The cool, fresh gazpacho sauce is the perfect accompaniment.

Preparation time 8 minutes
Cooking time 10–12 minutes

SERVES 4

4 turkey breast steaks
15ml/1 tbsp red pesto or tomato purée
4 chorizo sausages
salt and ground black pepper
For the gazpacho sauce
1 green pepper, seeded and chopped
1 red pepper, seeded and chopped
7.5cm/3in piece of cucumber
1 tomato
1 garlic clove, chopped
15ml/1 tbsp red wine vinegar
45ml/3 tbsp olive oil

1 To make the gazpacho sauce, place the peppers, cucumber, tomato, garlic, and vinegar in a food processor. Pour in 30ml/2 tbsp of the oil and process until almost smooth. Season to taste with salt and pepper and set aside.

2 If the turkey breast steaks are quite thick, place them between two sheets of clear film and beat them with the side of a rolling pin, to flatten them slightly.

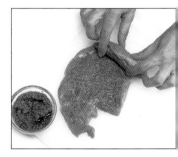

3 Spread the pesto or tomato purée over the turkey and then place a chorizo on each piece and roll up firmly. Preheat the grill.

4 Slice the rolls thickly and thread them on to skewers. Brush with the remaining oil and barbecue or grill for 10–12 minutes, turning once. Serve with the gazpacho sauce.

CHICKEN IN CREAMY ORANGE SAUCE

This sauce is deceptively creamy — in fact it is made with low-fat fromage frais, which is virtually fat-free. The brandy adds richness.

Preparation time 3–4 minutes
Cooking time 25 minutes

SERVES 4

8 skinless chicken thighs or
  drumsticks
45ml/3 tbsp brandy
300ml/ ½ pint/1¼ cups orange juice
3 spring onions, chopped
10ml/2 tsp cornflour
90ml/6 tbsp low-fat fromage frais
salt and ground black pepper
rice or pasta and green salad, to serve

1 Cook the chicken pieces without fat in a non-stick or heavy-based pan, turning until they are evenly browned.

2 Stir in the brandy, orange juice and spring onions. Bring to a boil, then cover, lower the heat and simmer for 15 minutes, or until the chicken is tender and fully cooked.

3 Blend the cornflour with a little water then stir the paste into the fromage frais. Stir this into the sauce and stir over a medium heat until the sauce boils and thickens.

4 Adjust the seasoning and serve with boiled rice or pasta and green salad.

COOK'S TIP
Skinless, boneless chicken thighs are perfect for this dish and a host of similar quick lunch or supper dishes. They cook rapidly and have plenty of flavour.

VARIATIONS
To make Turkey in Creamy Orange Sauce, substitute 4 turkey steaks for the chicken thighs or drumsticks.

TANDOORI CHICKEN KEBABS

This dish originates from the plains of the Punjab at the foot of the Himalayas. There food is traditionally cooked in clay ovens known as tandoors – hence the name.

Preparation time 18 minutes
Cooking time 10–12 minutes

SERVES 4
4 skinless, boneless chicken breasts, about 175g/6oz each
15ml/1 tbsp lemon juice
45ml/3 tbsp tandoori paste
45ml/3 tbsp natural yogurt
1 garlic clove, crushed
30ml/2 tbsp chopped fresh coriander
1 small onion, cut into wedges and separated into layers
a little oil, for brushing
salt and ground black pepper
fresh coriander sprigs, to garnish
pilau rice and naan bread, to serve

[1] Chop the chicken breasts into 2.5cm/1in cubes, place in a bowl and add the lemon juice, tandoori paste, yogurt, garlic, coriander and seasoning. Mix well. Cover and set aside for 15 minutes.

[2] Preheat the grill. Thread alternate pieces of chicken and onion on to four skewers.

[3] Brush the onion with a little oil, lay on a grill rack and cook under a high heat for 10–12 minutes, turning once. Garnish the kebabs with fresh coriander and serve at once with pilau rice and naan bread.

COOK'S TIP
You can make your own tandoori paste if you like, but the bought product is a boon to the busy cook.

CHINESE CHICKEN WITH CASHEW NUTS

Preparation time 20 minutes
Cooking time 10 minutes

SERVES 4
4 skinless, boneless chicken breasts, sliced into strips
3 garlic cloves, crushed
60ml/4 tbsp soy sauce
30ml/2 tbsp cornflour
225g/8oz dried egg noodles
45ml/3 tbsp sunflower oil
15ml/1 tbsp sesame oil
115g/4oz/1 cup roasted cashew nuts
6 spring onions, cut into 5cm/2in pieces and halved lengthways
spring onion curls and a little chopped red chilli, to garnish

[1] Place the chicken in a bowl with the garlic, soy sauce and cornflour. Stir to coat. Cover and chill for 15–18 minutes.

[2] Meanwhile, bring a pan of water to the boil and add the egg noodles. Turn off the heat and leave to stand for 5 minutes. Drain well and reserve.

[3] Heat the oils in a large frying pan or wok and add the chilled chicken and marinade juices. Stir-fry on a high heat for about 3–4 minutes, or until golden brown.

[4] Add the cashew nuts and spring onions to the pan or wok and stir-fry for 2–3 minutes.

[5] Add the drained noodles and stir-fry for a further 2 minutes. Toss the mixture well and serve immediately, garnished with the spring onion curls and chopped red chilli.

Turkey Sticks with Soured Cream Dip

Preparation time 10 minutes
Cooking time 20 minutes

Serves 4

*350g/12oz turkey fillets, or 2 skinless,
  boneless breasts*
*50g/2oz/1 cup fine fresh
  breadcrumbs*
1.5ml/ ¼ tsp paprika
1 egg
45ml/3 tbsp soured cream
*15ml/1 tbsp ready-made
  tomato sauce*
15ml/1 tbsp mayonnaise
salt and ground black pepper
green salad or vegetables, to serve

1 Preheat the oven to 190°C/
375°F/Gas 5. Cut the turkey
into strips. Mix the breadcrumbs
with paprika. Season with salt and
pepper. Beat the egg lightly in a
shallow bowl.

2 Dip the turkey into the egg,
then into the breadcrumbs,
until thoroughly and evenly coated.
Place on a baking sheet.

3 Bake the turkey for 20 minutes,
until crisp and golden. Turn
once during cooking.

4 To make the dip, mix the
soured cream, tomato sauce
and mayonnaise together in a small
bowl and season to taste. Serve the
turkey sticks with baked potatoes
and a green salad or crisp green
vegetables, accompanied by the dip.

Chicken, Bacon and Corn Kebabs

*Don't wait for barbecue weather to
serve these colourful kebabs.*

Preparation time 5 minutes
Cooking time 18–20 minutes

Serves 4

2 corn-on-the-cob
8 thick rindless back bacon rashers
8 brown cap mushrooms, halved
2 small chicken breast fillets
30ml/2 tbsp sunflower oil
15ml/1 tbsp lemon juice
15ml/1 tbsp maple syrup
salt and ground black pepper
salad, to serve

1 Cook the corn in boiling water
until tender, then drain and
set aside. Stretch the bacon rashers
with the back of a knife; cut each
in half. Wrap a piece around each
half mushroom.

2 Cut both the corn and chicken
into eight equal pieces. Mix the
oil, lemon juice, syrup and seasoning;
brush over the chicken.

3 Thread the corn, bacon-
wrapped mushrooms and
chicken pieces alternately on skewers
and brush with the lemon dressing.

4 Grill the kebabs for about
8–10 minutes, turning once and
basting occasionally with any extra
dressing. Serve hot with either a crisp
green or mixed leaf salad. If serving
the kebabs to children, slide the corn
and chicken off the skewers and
serve in pitta breads.

CHICKEN PAELLA

There are many variations of this basic recipe. Any seasonal vegetables can be added, as can mussels or clams. Serve straight from the pan.

Preparation time 3 minutes
Cooking time 25–27 minutes

SERVES 4

*4 chicken legs (thighs and
   drumsticks)
60ml/4 tbsp olive oil
1 large onion, finely chopped
1 garlic clove, crushed
5ml/1 tsp ground turmeric
115g/4oz chorizo sausage or
   smoked ham
225g/8oz/generous 1 cup long
   grain rice
600ml/1 pint/2 ½ cups chicken stock
4 tomatoes, peeled, seeded
   and chopped
1 red pepper, seeded and sliced
115g/4oz/1 cup frozen peas
salt and ground black pepper*

COOK'S TIP
Use chicken breasts if you prefer.

[1] Preheat the oven to 180°C/ 350°F/Gas 4. Cut the chicken legs in half. Heat the oil in a 30cm/12in paella pan or large flameproof casserole and brown the chicken pieces on both sides. Add the onion and garlic and stir in the turmeric. Cook for 2 minutes over a medium heat.

[2] Slice the sausage or dice the ham and add to the pan, with the rice and stock. Bring to the boil and season to taste, then lower the heat, cover and cook for 10 minutes.

[3] Remove from the heat and add the chopped tomatoes, sliced red pepper and frozen peas. Return to the heat and cook, stirring frequently for a further 10–15 minutes or until the chicken is tender and fully cooked and the rice has absorbed the stock.

Duck Breasts with Calvados

A plum and Calvados purée is the perfect accompaniment for glazed duck breasts with chicory.

Preparation time 5 minutes
Cooking time 25 minutes

Serves 4

15ml/1 tbsp lemon juice
4 heads of chicory
4 duck breasts, about 115g/4oz each
15ml/1 tbsp clear honey
5ml/1 tsp sunflower oil
salt and ground black pepper

For the purée

1 cooking apple, peeled, cored and sliced
175g/6oz plums, halved and stoned
15ml/1 tbsp soft light brown sugar
150ml/ ¼ pint/ ⅔ cup vegetable stock
45ml/3 tbsp Calvados
10ml/2 tsp sherry vinegar or red wine vinegar

1 Preheat the oven to 220°C/ 425°F/Gas 7. Make the fruit purée. Put the apple, plums, sugar and stock into a saucepan. Bring to the boil, lower the heat and simmer for 10 minutes until the fruit is very soft. Press the fruit through a strainer into a bowl.

2 Stir the lemon juice into a saucepan of lightly salted water and bring to the boil. Cut the heads of chicory lengthways into quarters and add to the pan. Cook for about 3 minutes, then drain and set aside.

3 Meanwhile, score the duck breasts using a sharp knife, then brush with honey and sprinkle with a little salt. Transfer to a baking sheet and bake for about 6 minutes.

Cook's Tip

Adding lemon juice to the water used for cooking the chicory helps to stop it discolouring.

4 Brush the chicory pieces with oil and place them alongside the duck. Bake for 6 minutes more.

5 Stir the Calvados and vinegar into the purée and season to taste with salt and pepper. Arrange the chicory pieces on a platter. Slice the duck breasts and fan them out on top of the chicory. Spoon the purée over and serve at once.

PEPPER STEAKS WITH CHIVE BUTTER AND BRANDY

Preparation time 4 minutes
Cooking time 12 minutes

SERVES 4

4 fillet or sirloin beef steaks, about
*   115–175g/4–6oz each*
45ml/3 tbsp olive oil
15ml/1 tbsp black and white
*   peppercorns, coarsely crushed*
1 garlic clove, halved
50g/2oz/ ¼ cup butter
30ml/2 tbsp brandy
250ml/8fl oz/1 cup ready-made
*   jellied beef stock*
salt and ground black pepper
tied chive bundles, to garnish
boiled new potatoes, to serve
For the chive butter
50g/2oz/ ¼ cup butter
45ml/3 tbsp snipped fresh chives

1 Make the chive butter. Beat the butter until soft, add the chives and season with salt and pepper. Beat until well mixed, then shape into a roll, wrap in foil and chill.

2 Brush the steaks with a little olive oil and press crushed peppercorns on to both sides.

3 Rub the cut surface of the garlic over a frying pan. Melt the butter in the remaining oil. When hot, add the steaks and fry quickly, allowing 3½–4 minutes on each side for medium-rare. Lift out with tongs, place on a serving plate and keep hot while you make the sauce.

4 Add the brandy and stock to the pan, boil rapidly until reduced by half, then season with salt and pepper to taste. Slice the chive butter and put a piece on top of each steak. Spoon a little sauce on to each plate. Garnish each steak with a chive bundle and serve with a simple vegetable accompaniment, such as boiled new potatoes.

HAM WITH MADEIRA SAUCE

Preparation time 4 minutes
Cooking time 26 minutes

SERVES 4

30ml/2 tbsp sunflower oil
2 ham or gammon steaks, about
*   115–175g/4–6oz each, fat snipped*
*   to prevent curling*
1 onion, sliced
175g/6oz/1½ cups button mushrooms
175g/6oz raw beetroot, peeled and
*   cut into thin sticks*
salt and ground black pepper
chopped fresh parsley, to garnish
For the sauce
25g/1oz/2 tbsp butter
1 large onion, chopped
1 rindless streaky bacon
*   rasher, chopped*
1 celery stick, diced
10ml/2 tsp plain flour
2 tomatoes, peeled and diced
15ml/1 tbsp tomato purée
300ml/ ½ pint/1¼ cups beef stock
15ml/1 tbsp chopped fresh parsley
30ml/2 tbsp Madeira

1 Make the sauce. Heat the butter and fry the onion, bacon and celery for 5 minutes until golden. Stir in the flour and cook until browned, then add the tomatoes, tomato purée, stock and parsley. Bring to the boil, then lower the heat and simmer while you cook the ham or gammon steaks.

COOK'S TIP
Straining the sauce through muslin will give a shiny, glossy finish.

2 Heat the oil in a frying pan and fry the ham or gammon steaks with the onion for about 10 minutes, stirring the onion occasionally. Turn the steaks over, add the mushrooms and fry for 10 minutes more, or until the steaks are fully cooked.

3 Meanwhile, cook the beetroot sticks in a pan of lightly salted boiling water for 5 minutes or until tender. Drain and keep hot.

4 Strain the sauce into a clean pan, stir in the Madeira and season to taste with salt and pepper.

5 Reheat the sauce, pour it over the steaks and serve with the mushrooms, onion and beetroot. Garnish with the parsley.

PAN-FRIED MEDITERRANEAN LAMB

The warm summery flavours of the Mediterranean are combined for a quick weekday meal.

Preparation time 4 minutes
Cooking time 24 minutes

SERVES 4
8 lean lamb cutlets
1 medium onion, thinly sliced
2 red peppers, seeded and sliced
400g/14oz can plum tomatoes
1 garlic clove, crushed
45ml/3 tbsp chopped fresh basil leaves
30ml/2 tbsp chopped black olives
salt and ground black pepper

1 Trim any excess fat from the lamb, then cook without fat in a non-stick pan until golden brown.

2 Add the onion and peppers to the pan. Cook, stirring, for a few minutes to soften, then add the plum tomatoes, garlic and basil.

3 Simmer for 20 minutes or until the lamb is tender. Stir in the olives, season, and serve.

VARIATIONS
This recipe would be equally good with skinless chicken breast fillets instead of the lamb cutlets. Or use cod steaks, which are very good with a robust tomato sauce.

BACON KOFTAS

These easy koftas are good for outdoor summer barbecues, served with lots of salad.

Preparation time 15 minutes
Cooking time 8–10 minutes

SERVES 4
225g/8oz rindless back bacon, coarsely chopped
75g/3oz/1 cup fresh wholemeal breadcrumbs
2 spring onions, chopped
15ml/1 tbsp chopped fresh parsley
finely grated rind of 1 lemon
1 egg white
ground black pepper
paprika
lemon rind and fresh parsley leaves, to garnish
lemon rice and salad, to serve

1 Place the bacon in a food processor together with the breadcrumbs, spring onions, parsley, lemon rind, egg white and pepper. Process the mixture until it is finely chopped and begins to bind together, but do not let it form a paste.

2 Divide the bacon mixture into eight even-size pieces and shape into long ovals around eight wooden or bamboo skewers. The easiest way to do this is to use your hands. Preheat the grill or barbecue.

3 Sprinkle the koftas with paprika and cook under the hot grill or on the barbecue for 8–10 minutes, turning occasionally, until browned and cooked through. Garnish with lemon rind and parsley leaves, then serve hot with lemon rice and salad.

COOK'S TIPS
Don't over-process the kofta mixture; it should be only just mixed. If you don't have a food processor, either mince the bacon, or chop it very finely by hand, then mix it with the rest of the ingredients.

Skewered Lamb with Cucumber Raita

Lamb is the most commonly used meat for Turkish kebabs, but lean beef or pork work equally well. For colour you can alternate pieces of pepper, lemon or onions, although this is not traditional.

Preparation time 15 minutes
Cooking time 10 minutes

Serves 4

900g/2lb lean boneless lamb
1 large onion, grated
3 bay leaves
5 thyme or rosemary sprigs
grated rind and juice of 1 lemon
2.5ml/ ½ tsp caster sugar
75ml/3fl oz/ ⅓ cup olive oil
salt and ground black pepper
sprigs of rosemary, to garnish
grilled lemon wedges, to serve

For the cucumber raita
½ cucumber
1 green chilli, seeded and chopped
300ml/ ½ pint/1¼ cups Greek yogurt
1.5ml/ ¼ tsp salt
1.5ml/ ¼ tsp ground cumin

1 To make the kebabs, cut the lamb into small chunks and put in a bowl. Mix together the grated onion, herbs, lemon rind and juice, sugar and oil, then add salt and pepper and pour over the lamb.

2 Mix the ingredients together and leave to marinate in the fridge while you make the raita.

COOK'S TIP
Cover the tips of wooden skewers with foil so they don't char.

3 Dice the cucumber finely and place in a bowl. Stir in the chopped chilli.

4 Add the yogurt, salt and ground cumin. Preheat the grill.

5 Drain the meat and thread it on skewers. Grill for 10 minutes until browned, turning twice. Garnish with the rosemary and grilled lemon wedges and serve with the raita.

PORK AND PINEAPPLE SATAY

This variation on the classic satay has added pineapple, but keeps the traditional coconut and peanut sauce. It is very easy to make and tastes delicious.

Preparation time 5–8 minutes
Cooking time 15 minutes

SERVES 4

500g/1¼ lb pork fillet
1 small onion, chopped
1 garlic clove, chopped
60ml/4 tbsp soy sauce
finely grated rind of ½ lemon
5ml/1 tsp ground cumin
5ml/1 tsp ground coriander
5ml/1 tsp ground turmeric
5ml/1 tsp dark muscovado sugar
225g/8oz can pineapple chunks, or
  1 small fresh pineapple, peeled
  and diced
parsley, to garnish

For the satay sauce
175ml/6fl oz/ ¾ cup coconut milk
115g/4oz/ ⅓ cup crunchy peanut
  butter
1 garlic clove, crushed
10ml/2 tsp soy sauce
5ml/1 tsp dark muscovado sugar

1 Trim any fat from the pork fillet and cut it in 2.5cm/1in cubes. Place the meat in a large bowl.

2 Place the onion, garlic, soy sauce, lemon rind, spices and sugar in a blender or food processor. Add two pieces of pineapple and process until the mixture is well combined and almost smooth.

3 Add the paste to the pork, tossing well to coat evenly. Thread the pieces of pork on to bamboo skewers, with the remaining pineapple chunks. Preheat the grill or light the barbecue.

COOK'S TIP
If you cannot buy coconut milk, look out for creamed coconut in a block. Stir a 50g/2oz piece in 150ml/¼ pint/⅔ cup boiling water until dissolved.

4 To make the sauce, pour the coconut milk into a small pan and stir in the peanut butter. Stir in all the remaining sauce ingredients and heat gently on the hob or over the barbecue, stirring until smooth and hot. Cover and keep warm.

5 Cook the pork and pineapple skewers under the grill or on a medium-hot barbecue for 10–12 minutes, turning occasionally, until golden brown and thoroughly cooked. Garnish with parsley and serve with the satay sauce.

Fried Rice with Pork

If liked, garnish the fried rice with strips of egg omelette.

Preparation time 16 minutes
Cooking time 10 minutes

Serves 4–6

225g/8oz/1 cups long grain rice
45ml/3 tbsp vegetable oil
1 onion, chopped
15ml/1 tbsp chopped garlic
115g/4oz pork, cut into small cubes
2 eggs, beaten
30ml/2 tbsp fish sauce
15ml/1 tbsp dark soy sauce
2.5 ml/ ½ tsp caster sugar

For the garnish
4 spring onions, finely sliced
2 red chillies, sliced
1 lime, cut into wedges

1. Cook the rice in boiling salted water for 11 minutes. Heat the oil in a wok or frying pan. Add the onion and garlic.

2. Cook the onion and garlic for 2 minutes, then add the pork and stir-fry until it is cooked.

3. Add the eggs and cook until scrambled into small lumps.

4. Add the rice and continue to stir and toss, to coat it with the oil and prevent it from sticking.

5. Stir in the fish sauce, soy sauce and sugar and mix well. Continue to fry until the rice is thoroughly heated. Tip into a bowl and garnish with sliced spring onion, red chillies and lime wedges. Top with a few strips of egg omelette, if you like.

BEEF AND MUSHROOM BURGERS

It's worth making your own burgers to cut down on fat — in these the meat is extended with mushrooms for extra fibre.

Preparation time 7 minutes
Cooking time 12–15 minutes

SERVES 4

150g/5oz/1¼ cups small mushrooms
1 small onion, chopped
450g/1lb lean minced beef
75g/3oz/1 cup fresh wholemeal
 breadcrumbs
5ml/1 tsp dried mixed herbs
15ml/1 tbsp tomato purée
plain flour, for shaping
salt and ground black pepper

1 Place the mushrooms and onion in a food processor and process until finely chopped. Add the beef, breadcrumbs, herbs and tomato purée. Season. Process until the mixture binds together but still has some texture.

2 Divide the mixture into 8–10 pieces, then press into burger shapes using lightly floured hands.

3 Cook the burgers in a non-stick frying pan, or under a hot grill for 12–15 minutes, turning once, until evenly cooked. Serve with relish and lettuce, in burger buns or pitta bread.

COOK'S TIP
The mixture is soft, so handle carefully and use a fish slice for turning to stop the burgers breaking during cooking.

PROSCIUTTO, MUSHROOM AND ARTICHOKE PIZZA

Here is a pizza full of rich and varied flavours. For a delicious variation use mixed cultivated and wild mushrooms.

Preparation time 3 minutes
Cooking time 20–25 minutes

SERVES 2–3
1 bunch spring onions
60ml/4 tbsp olive oil
225g/8oz/2 cups mushrooms, sliced
2 garlic cloves, chopped
1 pizza base, about
 25–30cm/10–12in diameter
8 slices prosciutto
4 bottled artichoke hearts in oil,
 drained and sliced
60ml/4 tbsp freshly grated Parmesan
salt and ground black pepper
thyme sprigs, to garnish

1 Preheat the oven to 220°C/ 425°F/Gas 7. Trim the spring onions, then chop all the white and some of the green stems.

2 Heat 30ml/2 tbsp of the oil in a frying pan. Add the spring onions, mushrooms and garlic and fry over a medium heat until all the juices have evaporated. Season and leave to cool.

3 Brush the pizza base with half the remaining oil. Arrange the prosciutto, mushroom mixture and artichoke hearts on top.

4 Sprinkle over the Parmesan, then drizzle over the remaining oil. Bake for 15–20 minutes. Garnish with thyme and serve.

MIXED SEAFOOD PIZZA

Here is a pizza that gives you the full flavour of the Mediterranean, ideal for a summer evening supper!

Preparation time 5 minutes
Cooking time 15–20 minutes

SERVES 3–4

1 pizza base, 25–30cm/10–12in diameter
30ml/2 tbsp olive oil
250ml/8fl oz/1 cup good quality pasta sauce
400g/14oz bag frozen mixed cooked seafood, thawed
3 garlic cloves
30ml/2 tbsp chopped fresh parsley
30ml/2 tbsp freshly grated Parmesan cheese, to serve

VARIATION

If you prefer, this pizza can be made with either mussels or prawns on their own, or any combination of your favourite seafood.

1. Preheat the oven to 220°C/425°F/Gas 7. Lightly brush the top of the pizza base with about 15ml/1 tbsp of the olive oil.

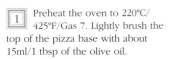

2. Spread over the pasta sauce. Bake for 10 minutes.

3. Pat the seafood dry using kitchen paper, then arrange on top of the pizza.

4. Finely chop the garlic and scatter it evenly over the surface, then sprinkle over the chopped fresh parsley.

5. Drizzle the remaining oil over the top and return the pizza to the oven. Bake for 5–10 minutes more, until the seafood is warmed through and the base is crisp and golden. Sprinkle generously with freshly grated Parmesan cheese and serve immediately.

PINEAPPLE CURRY WITH PRAWNS AND MUSSELS

The delicate sweet and sour flavour of this curry comes from the pineapple and although it seems an odd combination, it is rather delicious. Use the freshest shellfish that you can find.

Preparation time 15 minutes
Cooking time 10 minutes

SERVES 4–6
600ml/1 pint/2½ cups coconut milk
30ml/2 tbsp red curry paste
30ml/2 tbsp fish sauce
15ml/1 tbsp granulated sugar
225g/8oz raw king prawns, shelled
    and deveined
450g/1lb live mussels, cleaned and
    beards removed
175g/6oz fresh pineapple, finely
    crushed or chopped
5 kaffir lime leaves
2 red chillies, chopped, and fresh
    coriander leaves, to garnish

[1] In a large saucepan, bring half the coconut milk to the boil. Heat, stirring, until it separates.

[2] Add the red curry paste and cook until fragrant. Add the fish sauce and sugar and continue to cook for about 1 minute.

Stir in the rest of the coconut milk and bring back to the boil. Add the king prawns, mussels and pineapple. Tear the kaffir lime leaves into pieces and stir them into the mixture.

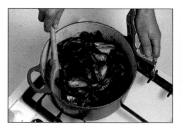

[4] Reheat until boiling, then lower the heat and simmer for 3–5 minutes, until the prawns are cooked and the mussels have opened. Remove any mussels that have not opened and discard. Spoon into a serving dish, garnish with chopped red chillies and coriander leaves and serve.

COOK'S TIP
To save time, use drained canned crushed pineapple instead of fresh.

CURRIED PRAWNS IN COCONUT MILK

Preparation time 4 minutes
Cooking time 22 minutes

SERVES 4–6
600ml/1 pint/2½ cups coconut milk
30ml/2 tbsp yellow curry paste (see
    Cook's Tip)
15ml/1 tbsp fish sauce
2.5ml/½ tsp salt
5ml/1 tsp granulated sugar
450g/1lb raw king prawns, shelled,
    tails left intact and deveined
225g/8oz cherry tomatoes
juice of ½ lime, to serve
For the garnish
2 red chillies, cut into strips
fresh coriander leaves

[1] Put half the coconut milk into a pan or wok and bring to the boil over a medium heat.

[2] Add the yellow curry paste to the warmed coconut milk, stir until it dissolves, then simmer for about 10 minutes. Add the fish sauce, salt, sugar and remaining coconut milk. Simmer for 5 minutes more or until the sauce thickens.

[3] Add the prawns and cherry tomatoes. Simmer very gently for about 5 minutes until the prawns are pink and tender.

[4] Serve sprinkled with lime juice and garnished with chillies and coriander leaves.

COOK'S TIP
To make yellow curry paste, process together 6–8 yellow chillies, 1 chopped lemon grass stalk, 4 peeled shallots, 4 garlic cloves, 15ml/1 tbsp peeled chopped fresh root ginger, 5ml/1 tsp coriander seeds, 5ml/1 tsp mustard powder, 5ml/1 tsp salt, 2.5ml/½ tsp ground cinnamon, 15ml/1 tbsp light brown sugar and 30ml/2 tbsp oil in a blender or food processor. When a paste has formed, transfer to a glass jar and keep in the fridge.

PAN-FRIED TROUT WITH HAZELNUTS

Hazelnuts make an interesting topping for trout.

Preparation and cooking time 30 minutes

SERVES 4

50g/2oz/ ½ cup shelled hazelnuts, chopped
65g/2 ½ oz/ ⅓ cup butter
4 trout, about 275g/10oz each
30ml/2 tbsp lemon juice
salt and ground black pepper
lemon slices and flat leaf parsley sprigs, to garnish

1 Preheat the grill. Toast the hazelnuts in a single layer, stirring frequently, until the skins split. Then tip them on to a clean dish towel and rub to remove the skins. Leave the hazelnuts to cool, then chop them coarsely.

2 Heat 50g/2oz/¼ cup of the butter in a large frying pan. Season the trout inside and out, then fry two at a time for 12 minutes, turning once, until the trout are brown and the flesh flakes easily when tested with the tip of a sharp knife.

COOK'S TIP
You can use a microwave to prepare the nuts, spread them in a shallow dish and cook on full power until the skins split. Watch them closely, as they scorch readily.

3 Drain the cooked trout on kitchen paper, then transfer to a warm serving plate and keep hot while frying the remaining trout in the same way. (If your frying pan is large enough, you could, of course, cook the trout in one batch.) When batch frying, it may be necessary to add a little more butter to the frying pan.

4 Add the remaining butter to the frying pan, then add the hazelnuts and fry them until evenly browned. Stir the lemon juice into the pan and mix well, then quickly pour the buttery sauce over the trout and serve at once, garnished with slices of lemon and flat leaf parsley sprigs.

PASTA WITH SCALLOPS IN TOMATO SAUCE

Preparation time 6 minutes
Cooking time 17 minutes

SERVES 4
*450g/1lb pasta, such as fettucine
or linguine*
30ml/2 tbsp olive oil
2 garlic cloves, finely chopped
*450g/1lb scallops, sliced in half
horizontally*
30ml/2 tbsp chopped fresh basil
salt and ground black pepper
fresh basil sprigs, to garnish
For the sauce
30ml/2 tbsp olive oil
1/2 onion, finely chopped
1 garlic clove, finely chopped
salt, to taste
2 x 400g/14 oz cans peeled tomatoes

VARIATION
Substitute 6 peeled fresh plum tomatoes
for the canned tomatoes, if you like.

1 | To make the sauce, heat the oil in a non-stick frying pan. Add the onion, garlic and a little salt, and cook over a medium heat for about 3 minutes, stirring occasionally.

2 | Add the tomatoes, with their juice, and crush with a fork. Bring to the boil, then reduce the heat and simmer while you cook the pasta.

3 | Bring a large pan of salted water to the boil. Add the pasta and cook for about 10 minutes, until just tender.

4 | Meanwhile, combine the oil and garlic in another non-stick frying pan and cook for about 30 seconds, until just sizzling. Add the scallops and 2.5ml/1/2 tsp salt and toss over a high heat for about 3 minutes until they are cooked.

5 | Reheat the tomato sauce, add the scallops and season to taste. Keep warm over a very low heat.

6 | Drain the pasta, rinse under hot water, and drain again. Tip into a bowl and toss with the scallop sauce and the basil. Garnish with basil sprigs and serve.

SOLE GOUJONS WITH LIME MAYONNAISE

This simple dish can be rustled up very quickly. It makes an excellent light lunch or supper.

Preparation time 5–7 minutes
Cooking time 10 minutes

SERVES 4
250ml/8fl oz/1 cup mayonnaise
1 small garlic clove, crushed
10ml/2 tsp capers, rinsed
and chopped
10ml/2 tsp chopped gherkins
finely grated rind of ¹/₂ lime
10ml/2 tsp lime juice
15ml/1 tbsp chopped fresh coriander
675g/1¹/₂ lb sole fillets, skinned
2 eggs, beaten
115g/4oz/2 cups fresh white
breadcrumbs
oil, for deep-frying
salt and ground black pepper
lime wedges, to serve

1 To make the lime mayonnaise, mix together the mayonnaise, garlic, capers, gherkins, lime rind and juice and chopped coriander. Season with salt and pepper. Transfer to a serving bowl.

2 Cut the sole fillets into finger-length strips. Dip into the beaten egg, then into the fresh white breadcrumbs.

3 Heat the oil in a deep-fat fryer to 180°C/350°F. Add the fish in batches and fry until golden brown and crisp. Drain on kitchen paper.

4 Pile the goujons on to warmed serving plates and serve with the lime wedges for squeezing over. Hand the lime mayonnaise around separately.

SPICY FISH RÖSTI

Serve these fish cakes crisp and hot for lunch with a green salad.

Preparation time 4 minutes
Cooking time 20 minutes

SERVES 4
350g/12oz large, firm
waxy potatoes
350g/12oz salmon or cod fillet,
skinned, stray bones removed
3–4 spring onions, finely chopped
5ml/1 tsp grated fresh root ginger
30ml/2 tbsp chopped fresh
coriander
10ml/2 tsp lemon juice
45ml/3 tbsp sunflower oil
salt and cayenne pepper
lemon wedges, to serve

1 Cook the potatoes with their skins on in a pan of boiling salted water for 10 minutes. Drain and leave to cool for a few minutes.

2 Meanwhile, finely chop the salmon or cod fillet and put into a bowl. Stir in the spring onions, ginger, coriander and lemon juice. Season with salt and cayenne.

3 When the potatoes are cool enough to handle, peel off the skins and grate the potatoes coarsely. Gently stir the grated potato into the fish mixture.

4 Form the fish and potato mixture into 12 cakes.

5 Heat the oil in a large frying pan, and, when hot, fry the fish cakes a few at a time for 3 minutes on each side, until golden brown and crisp. Drain on kitchen paper. Serve hot with lemon wedges for squeezing over. Garnish with sprigs of fresh coriander, if you like.

TUNA STEAKS WITH PAN-FRIED PLUM TOMATOES

Preparation time 15–20 minutes
Cooking time 8–10 minutes

SERVES 2

2 tuna steaks, about 175g/6oz each
90ml/6 tbsp olive oil
30ml/2 tbsp lemon juice
2 garlic cloves, chopped
5ml/1 tsp chopped fresh thyme
4 drained, canned anchovy fillets,
  finely chopped
225g/8oz plum tomatoes, halved
30ml/2 tbsp chopped fresh parsley
4–6 black olives, pitted and chopped
ground black pepper
crusty bread, to serve

COOK'S TIP

If you are unable to find fresh tuna
steaks, you could replace them with
salmon fillets, if you like – just cook
them for one or two minutes more on
each side.

[1] Place the tuna steaks in a
shallow non-metallic dish. Mix
60ml/4 tbsp of the oil with the lemon
juice, garlic, thyme, anchovies and
pepper. Pour this mixture over the
tuna and leave to marinate for at least
15 minutes, longer if possible.

[2] Lift the tuna from the marinade
and place on a grill rack. Grill
for 4 minutes on each side, or until
the tuna feels firm to touch, basting
with the marinade.

[3] Meanwhile, heat the remaining
oil in a frying pan. Fry the
tomatoes briefly on each side.

[4] Divide the tomatoes equally
between two serving plates and
scatter over the chopped parsley and
olives. Top each with a tuna steak.

[5] Add the remaining marinade to
the pan juices and warm
through. Pour over the tomatoes and
tuna steaks and serve at once with
crusty bread for mopping up the
delectable juices.

GRILLED SEA BASS WITH FENNEL

Fish and fennel are a famous — and delicious — combination.

Preparation time 2 minutes
Cooking time 28 minutes

SERVES 6–8
1 sea bass, weighing 1.75kg/4–4½ lb, cleaned
60–90ml/4–6 tbsp olive oil
10–15ml/2–3 tsp fennel seeds
2 large fennel bulbs
60ml/4 tbsp Pernod
salt and ground black pepper

 1 With a sharp knife, make three or four deep cuts in both sides of the fish. Brush the fish with olive oil and season with salt and pepper. Sprinkle the fennel seeds in the stomach cavity and cuts. Set aside.

2 Trim the fennel bulbs, saving any fronds. Quarter the bulbs, remove the cores and slice thinly.

3 Preheat the grill. Put the slices of fennel in a flameproof dish or on the grill rack and brush with oil. Grill for 4 minutes on each side until tender. Transfer to a large platter and keep hot.

4 Place the fish on the oiled grill rack and position about 10–13cm/4–5in away from the heat. Grill for 10 minutes on each side, brushing with oil occasionally.

5 Transfer the fish to the platter on top of the fennel. Garnish with fennel fronds. Heat the Pernod in a small pan, light it and pour it, flaming, over the fish. Serve at once.

KASHMIRI COCONUT FISH CURRY

Preparation time 6 minutes
Cooking time 20–24 minutes

SERVES 4
30ml/2 tbsp vegetable oil
2 onions, sliced
1 green pepper, seeded and sliced
1 garlic clove, crushed
1 dried chilli, seeded and chopped
5ml/1 tsp ground coriander
5ml/1 tsp ground cumin
2.5ml/ ½ tsp ground turmeric
2.5ml/ ½ tsp hot chilli powder
2.5ml/ ½ tsp garam masala
15ml/1 tbsp plain flour
115g/4oz creamed coconut, chopped
600ml/1 pint/2½ cups boiling water
675g/1½ lb haddock fillet
4 tomatoes, peeled, seeded
    and chopped
15ml/1 tbsp lemon juice
30ml/2 tbsp ground almonds
30ml/2 tbsp double cream
fresh coriander sprigs, to garnish
naan bread and boiled rice, to serve

1 Heat the oil in a large saucepan and add the onions, pepper and garlic. Cook for 6–7 minutes, until the onions and peppers have softened. Stir in the chopped dried chilli, all the ground spices and the flour. Cook for 1 minute.

2 Dissolve the coconut in the boiling water and stir into the spicy vegetable mixture. Bring to the boil, cover, lower the heat and simmer gently for 6 minutes.

3 Skin the fish and chop the flesh roughly. Add the fish and tomatoes to the pan and cook for about 5–6 minutes, or until the fish has turned opaque. Uncover and gently stir in the lemon juice, ground almonds and cream. Season well, garnish with coriander and serve with naan bread and rice.

VARIATIONS
Replace the haddock with any firm fleshed white fish such as cod or whiting. Stir in a few cooked, peeled prawns, if you like.

MUSSELS WITH WINE AND GARLIC

This famous French dish is better known as moules marinière.

Preparation time 10 minutes
Cooking time 12 minutes

SERVES 4
1.75kg/4–4½ lb live mussels
15ml/1 tbsp oil
25g/1oz/2 tbsp butter
1 small onion or 2 shallots, finely
    chopped
2 garlic cloves, finely chopped
150ml/¼ pint/⅔ cup dry white wine
    or cider
fresh parsley sprigs
ground black pepper
30ml/2 tbsp chopped fresh parsley,
    to garnish
French bread, to serve

1 Check that the mussels are closed. (Throw away any that are cracked or won't close when tapped.) Scrape the shells under cold running water and pull off the hairy beard attached to the hinge of the shell. Rinse well several times.

2 Heat the oil and butter in a large pan, add the onions or shallots and garlic and fry for 3–4 minutes, until softened.

3 Pour on the wine or cider and add the parsley sprigs. Stir well, bring to the boil, then add the mussels. Cover and cook for about 5–7 minutes, shaking the pan once or twice until the shells open (throw away any that stay shut).

4 Tip the mussels and their juices into a bowl and top with chopped parsley and black pepper. Serve with hot French bread.

SEAFOOD SALAD PROVENÇALE

You can't beat this salad for an almost instant starter or main course, and it is the perfect choice for a buffet table as it keeps so well.

Preparation time 25 minutes
Cooking time Nil

SERVES 4
350g/12oz mixed cooked seafood,
   such as peeled prawns, mussels,
   winkles and crabsticks
30ml/2 tbsp ready-made tomato
   sauce
1 garlic clove, crushed
60ml/4 tbsp pimiento antipasto
60ml/4 tbsp artichoke antipasto
½ yellow pepper, seeded and sliced
lemon juice, to taste
30ml/2 tbsp white wine (optional)
salt and ground black pepper
30ml/2 tbsp chopped fresh parsley
   and whole prawns, to garnish

| 1 | Toss the seafood in the tomato sauce, add the garlic and leave to stand for 5–10 minutes.

| 2 | Mix the pimiento antipasto with the artichoke antipasto, the yellow pepper, lemon juice and wine, if using.

| 3 | Stir in the seafood mixture, season to taste, and chill for 15 minutes or longer. Sprinkle with parsley and garnish with prawns before serving.

MONKFISH AND POTATO KEBABS

Monkfish is a good, firm fish so it works well for kebabs and can be cooked over a fierce heat.

Preparation time 20–25 minutes
Cooking time 4–5 minutes

SERVES 4
12–16 small new potatoes
12–16 seedless grapes
10cm/4in piece cucumber, cubed
275–350g/10–12oz monkfish tail,
   boned and cubed
75g/3oz/⅓ cup butter
grated rind and juice of 1 lime
5ml/1 tsp grated fresh root ginger
15ml/1 tbsp chopped fresh parsley
45–60ml/3–4 tbsp white wine
salt and ground black pepper
salad, to serve

| 1 | Boil the potatoes, then arrange on skewers with the grapes, cucumber and monkfish cubes.

| 2 | Melt two-thirds of the butter and stir in the lime rind and juice, ginger, seasoning and half the parsley. Brush over the kebabs.

| 3 | Preheat the grill and cook the kebabs, in a dish or on a sheet of foil to catch all the juices, for 2 minutes on each side.

| 4 | When cooked, transfer the kebabs to hot plates while heating the juices with the wine and the remaining butter. Check the seasoning, sprinkle the kebabs with parsley and serve with a salad and the tangy lime sauce.

LEMON GRASS PRAWNS ON CRISP NOODLE CAKE

Preparation time 10 minutes
Cooking time 15 minutes

SERVES 4

300g/11oz thin egg noodles
60ml/4 tbsp vegetable oil
500g/1¼ lb raw king prawns, peeled
  and deveined
2.5ml/ ½ tsp ground coriander
15ml/1 tbsp ground turmeric
2 garlic cloves, finely chopped
2 slices fresh root ginger,
  finely chopped
2 lemon grass stalks, finely chopped
2 shallots, finely chopped
15ml/1 tbsp tomato purée
250ml/8fl oz/1 cup coconut cream
15–30ml/1–2 tbsp fresh lime juice
15–30ml/1–2 tbsp fish sauce
4–6 kaffir lime leaves (optional)
1 cucumber, peeled, seeded and cut
  into 5cm/2in batons
1 tomato, seeded and cut into strips
2 red chillies, seeded and finely sliced
salt and ground black pepper
finely sliced spring onions, and a few
  coriander sprigs, to garnish

1 | Cook the egg noodles in a saucepan of boiling water until just tender. Drain, rinse under cold running water and drain well.

2 | Heat 15ml/1 tbsp of the oil in a large frying pan. Add the noodles, distributing them evenly, and fry for 4–5 minutes until crisp and golden. Turn the noodle cake over and fry the other side. Alternatively, make four individual cakes. Keep hot.

3 | Toss the prawns with the ground spices, garlic, ginger and lemon grass. Season.

4 | Heat the remaining oil in a large frying pan. Fry the shallots for 1 minute, then add the prawns and fry for 2 minutes more. Lift out the prawns.

5 | Stir the tomato purée and coconut cream into the mixture remaining in the pan. Stir in lime juice to taste and season with the fish sauce. Bring the sauce to a simmer, return the prawns to the sauce, then add the kaffir lime leaves, if using, and the cucumber. Simmer gently until the prawns are cooked and the sauce is a nice coating consistency.

6 | Add the tomato, stir until just warmed through, then add the chillies. Serve on top of the crisp noodle cake(s), garnished with sliced spring onions and coriander sprigs.

SMOKED TROUT PILAFF

Preparation time 5 minutes
Cooking time 25 minutes

SERVES 4

*225g/8oz/1¼ cups white basmati or
    long grain rice
40g/1½oz/3 tbsp butter
2 onions, sliced into rings
1 garlic clove, crushed
2 bay leaves
2 whole cloves
2 green cardamom pods
2 cinnamon sticks
5ml/1 tsp cumin seeds
600ml/1 pint/2½ cups boiling water
4 smoked trout fillets, skinned
50g/2oz/½ cup slivered almonds,
    toasted
50g/2oz/⅓ cup seedless raisins
30ml/2 tbsp chopped fresh parsley
mango chutney and poppadoms,
    to serve*

1 Wash the rice thoroughly in several changes of water and drain well. Melt the butter in a large frying pan and fry the onions until well browned, stirring often.

2 Add the garlic, bay leaves and spices. Stir-fry for 1 minute.

3 Stir in the rice, then the boiling water. Bring to the boil. Cover the pan, reduce the heat and cook very gently for 20 minutes, until the water has been absorbed and the rice is tender.

4 Flake the smoked trout and add to the pan with the almonds and raisins. Fork through. Replace the lid and allow the smoked trout to warm for a few minutes. Scatter over the parsley and serve with mango chutney and poppadoms.

CRUNCHY-TOPPED COD

Preparation time 4 minutes
Cooking time 15–20 minutes

SERVES 4

4 pieces cod fillet, about 115g/4oz
  each, skinned
2 medium tomatoes, sliced
75g/3oz/1 cup fresh wholemeal
  breadcrumbs
30ml/2 tbsp chopped fresh parsley
5ml/1 tsp sunflower oil
finely grated rind and juice of
  ½ lemon
salt and ground black pepper

1 Preheat the oven to 200°C/
400°F/Gas 6. Arrange the cod
fillets in a wide, ovenproof dish.

2 Arrange the tomato slices on
top. Mix the breadcrumbs, fresh
parsley, oil, lemon rind and juice.
Season to taste.

3 Spoon the crumb mixture
evenly over the fish, then bake
for 15–20 minutes. Serve hot.

COOK'S TIP
Choose firm, ripe tomatoes with plenty
of flavour. In the summer you may be
fortunate enough to find fresh plum
tomatoes, which are perfect for this
tasty dish.

CRUMBLY FISH AND PRAWN BAKE

*This fish pie is very easy to make.
For a more economical version, omit
the prawns and replace with more
fish fillet.*

Preparation time 5 minutes
Cooking time 25 minutes

SERVES 4

350g/12oz haddock fillet, skinned
30ml/2 tbsp cornflour
115g/4oz cooked, peeled prawns
200g/7oz can sweetcorn, drained
75g/3oz/¾ cup frozen peas
150ml/¼ pint/⅔ cup milk
150g/5oz/⅔ cup fromage frais
75g/3oz/1 cup fresh wholemeal
  breadcrumbs
40g/1½oz/½ cup grated Cheddar
  cheese
salt and ground black pepper
fresh vegetables, to serve

1 Preheat the oven to 190°C/
375°F/Gas 5. Cut the fish fillets
into bite-size pieces and toss in
the cornflour.

2 Mix together the fish, prawns,
sweetcorn and peas in a dish.
Combine the milk and fromage frais,
season and pour into the dish.

3 Mix together the breadcrumbs
and grated cheese, then spoon
evenly over the top. Bake for about
25 minutes, or until golden brown.
Serve hot, with fresh vegetables.

COOK'S TIP
This quick recipe can be prepared well
ahead and chilled – keep the breadcrumb topping separately, sprinkling
it over the fish and prawn mixture just
before baking.

SALMON, COURGETTE AND SWEETCORN FRITTATA

A delicious and exciting change from an omelette, but almost as fast, serve this filling frittata with a mixed tomato and pepper salad and warm wholemeal or Granary bread rolls.

Preparation time 10 minutes
Cooking time 16 minutes

SERVES 4–6

10ml/2 tsp olive oil
1 onion, chopped
175g/6oz courgettes, thinly sliced
225g/8oz boiled potatoes in their skins, diced
3 eggs, plus 2 egg whites
30ml/2 tbsp milk
200g/7oz can pink salmon in brine, drained and flaked
200g/7oz can sweetcorn, drained
10ml/2 tsp dried mixed herbs
50g/2oz/ ½ cup finely grated mature Cheddar cheese
salt and ground black pepper
chopped fresh mixed herbs and basil leaves, to garnish
thinly sliced tomatoes and strips of red, yellow and green pepper, to serve

1 Heat the oil in a large non-stick frying pan. Add the onion and fry for 2 minutes over a medium heat, then stir in the thinly sliced courgettes and cook for 3 minutes, stirring the mixture occasionally.

2 Add the potatoes and cook for 5 minutes, stirring occasionally.

3 Beat the eggs, egg whites and milk together, add the salmon, sweetcorn, herbs and seasoning and pour the mixture evenly over the vegetables.

4 Cook over a medium heat until the eggs are beginning to set and are golden brown underneath.

5 Preheat the grill. Sprinkle the cheese over and place the frittata under a medium heat until the cheese has melted and the top is golden brown.

6 Sprinkle with chopped fresh herbs, cut into wedges and serve immediately, garnished with basil leaves and accompanied by sliced tomatoes and mixed peppers.

COOK'S TIP
For a reduced-fat version of the frittata, use skimmed milk and Edam or reduced-fat Cheddar cheese.

MIXED VEGETABLES WITH AROMATIC SEEDS

Transform a selection of everyday vegetables by tossing them with a mixture of fried ginger and aromatic seeds.

Preparation time 6 minutes
Cooking time 24 minutes

SERVES 4–6

675g/1½ lb small new potatoes
1 small cauliflower
175g/6oz French beans
115g/4oz/1 cup frozen peas
small piece of fresh root ginger
30ml/2 tbsp sunflower oil
10ml/2 tsp cumin seeds
10ml/2 tsp black mustard seeds
30ml/2 tbsp sesame seeds
juice of 1 lemon
ground black pepper
fresh coriander, to garnish (optional)

1 Scrub the potatoes, cut the cauliflower into small florets, and trim and halve the French beans. Cook the vegetables in separate pans of lightly salted boiling water until tender, allowing 15–20 minutes for the potatoes, 8 minutes for the cauliflower and 4 minutes for the beans and peas. Drain thoroughly.

2 Using a small, sharp knife, peel and finely chop the fresh ginger. Heat the oil. Add the ginger and seeds. Fry until they start to pop.

3 Add the vegetables and stir-fry for 2–3 minutes. Sprinkle over the lemon juice and season with pepper. Garnish with fresh coriander, if using.

COOK'S TIP
Other vegetables could be used, such as courgettes, leeks or broccoli. Buy whatever looks freshest and do not store vegetables for long periods as their vitamin content will deteriorate.

EGGS WITH SPINACH AND CHEESE SAUCE

To save time, use 450g/1lb thawed frozen spinach. There's no need to pre-cook it; just squeeze out the surplus liquid and add it in step 4.

Preparation time 16 minutes
Cooking time 10–12 minutes

SERVES 4

1kg/2¼lb fresh spinach, stalks removed
40g/1½oz/3 tbsp butter
45ml/3 tbsp plain flour
300ml/½ pint/1¼ cups milk
75g/3oz/¾ cup grated mature Cheddar cheese
pinch of mustard powder
large pinch of freshly grated nutmeg
4 hard-boiled eggs, peeled and halved lengthways
salt and ground black pepper

1 Wash but do not dry the spinach, then place in a large saucepan with just the water clinging to the leaves. Cover and cook for 1–2 minutes until the spinach is just wilted and no free liquid is visible. Tip the spinach into a sieve and squeeze out as much liquid as possible, then chop it.

2 Melt 25g/1oz/2 tbsp of the butter in a saucepan, stir in the flour and cook for 1 minute. Gradually add the milk, stirring until the sauce boils and thickens. Lower the heat and simmer for 4 minutes.

3 Remove the pan from the heat and stir in 50g/2oz/½ cup of the cheese, the mustard and seasoning. Preheat the grill.

4 Melt the remaining butter in a small saucepan, then stir in the spinach, nutmeg and seasoning and warm through. Transfer the spinach to a shallow baking dish and arrange the egg halves on top in a single layer.

5 Pour the sauce over the eggs, sprinkle with the remaining cheese and place under the grill until golden and bubbling.

POTATO AND RED PEPPER FRITTATA

Fresh herbs make all the difference in this simple but delicious recipe.

Preparation time 4 minutes
Cooking time 21–26 minutes

SERVES 3–4
450g/1lb small new potatoes,
  scrubbed
6 eggs
30ml/2 tbsp chopped fresh mint
30ml/2 tbsp olive oil
1 onion, chopped
2 garlic cloves, crushed
2 red peppers, seeded and
  roughly chopped
salt and ground black pepper
fresh mint sprigs, to garnish

1 Bring a saucepan of lightly salted water to the boil and cook the potatoes for 15–20 minutes, until just tender. Drain and cool briefly, then slice thickly.

2 Whisk the eggs and mint in a bowl. Season to taste.

3 Heat the oil in a large frying pan. Fry the onion, garlic, peppers and potatoes for 5 minutes.

4 Pour the egg mixture over the vegetables and stir gently.

5 As it cooks, push the cooked mixture into the centre so the uncooked egg runs on to the base.

6 When the egg mixture is just set, place the pan under a hot grill for 2–3 minutes, until golden brown. Cut into wedges and serve, garnished with sprigs of mint.

POTATO CAKES WITH GOAT'S CHEESE

Preparation time 8–10 minutes
Cooking time 14–19 minutes

SERVES 4

450g/1lb potatoes
10ml/2 tsp chopped fresh thyme
1 garlic clove, crushed
2 spring onions, chopped
30ml/2 tbsp olive oil
50g/2oz/ ¼ cup butter
2 x 65g/2½ oz firm goat's cheese
salt and ground black pepper
salad leaves, such as curly endive,
  radicchio and lamb's lettuce, tossed
  in walnut dressing, to serve
fresh thyme sprigs, to garnish

1 Peel and coarsely grate the potatoes. Using your hands squeeze out all the excess moisture, then carefully combine with the chopped thyme, garlic, spring onions and seasoning.

2 Heat half the oil and butter in a non-stick frying-pan. Add two large spoonfuls of potato mixture, spacing them well apart, and press firmly with a spatula. Cook for 3–4 minutes on each side until golden.

3 Drain the potato cakes on kitchen paper and keep hot. Make two more potato cakes in the same way with the remaining mixture. Meanwhile, preheat the grill.

4 Cut the cheese in half horizontally and place one half, cut side up, on each potato cake. Grill for 2–3 minutes until golden. Serve the potato cakes with the salad leaves. Garnish with thyme sprigs and serve at once.

GARLIC BAKED TOMATOES

If you can find them, use Italian plum tomatoes, which have a warm, slightly sweet flavour. For large numbers of people you could use whole cherry tomatoes, tossed several times during cooking.

Preparation time 2 minutes
Cooking time 15–25 minutes

SERVES 4
40g/1½oz/3 tbsp unsalted butter
1 large garlic clove, crushed
5ml/1 tsp finely grated orange rind
2 large beefsteak tomatoes or 4 firm
   plum tomatoes
salt and ground black pepper
shredded fresh basil leaves, to garnish

1 Soften the butter and blend with the crushed garlic, grated orange rind and seasoning. Chill for a few minutes.

2 Preheat the oven to 200°C/ 400°F/Gas 6. Cut the tomatoes in half crossways.

3 Place the tomatoes in an ovenproof dish and spread the butter equally over each tomato half.

4 Bake the tomatoes in the oven for 15–25 minutes, depending on the size of the tomato halves, until just tender. Serve sprinkled with the basil leaves.

COOK'S TIP
Quick cooks will find it useful to keep a supply of garlic butter in the freezer. Make it up as described left, or omit the orange rind and add chopped fresh parsley. Freeze in thick slices or chunks ready to use, or roll into a sausage shape and wrap in foil, then cut into slices when partly thawed. Wrap garlic butter very well to prevent it from tainting other foods.

LEMON CARROT SALAD

Nothing could be quicker or easier than this tangy, colourful and refreshing salad. You can grate the carrots by hand, but a food processor with a grating plate will be even faster and more efficient.

Preparation time 25–30 minutes
Cooking time Nil

SERVES 4–6
450g/1lb small, young carrots
grated rind and juice of ½ lemon
15ml/1 tbsp soft light brown sugar
60ml/4 tbsp sunflower oil
5ml/1 tsp hazelnut or sesame oil
5ml/1 tsp chopped fresh oregano, or
   pinch of dried oregano
salt and ground black pepper

1 Finely grate the carrots and place them in a large bowl. Stir in the lemon rind, 15–30ml/1–2 tbsp of the lemon juice, the sugar, sunflower and hazelnut or sesame oils, and mix well.

2 Add more lemon juice and seasoning to taste, sprinkle on the oregano, toss and leave the salad for 20 minutes before serving.

COOK'S TIP
Other root vegetables could be used in this salad. For instance, you could try replacing half the carrot with swede, or use celeriac or kohlrabi instead.

RISOTTO ALLA MILANESE

Italian risottos have a distinctive creamy texture that is achieved by using arborio rice, a short grain rice that absorbs plenty of stock, but at the same time retains its texture. This risotto, scattered with cheese and gremolata, makes a delicious light meal or accompaniment to a meaty stew or casserole.

Preparation and
cooking time 30 minutes

SERVES 4

5ml/1 tsp (or 1 sachet) saffron
   strands
15ml/1 tbsp boiling water
25g/1oz/2 tbsp butter
1 large onion, finely chopped
275g/10oz/1½ cups arborio
   (risotto) rice
150ml/ ¼ pint/⅔ cup dry
   white wine
1 litre/1¾ pints/4 cups vegetable stock
salt and ground black pepper
Parmesan cheese shavings or grated
   Parmesan, to serve

For the gremolata
2 garlic cloves, crushed
60ml/4 tbsp chopped fresh parsley
finely grated rind of 1 lemon

1 Start by making the gremolata. Combine the crushed garlic, chopped parsley and grated lemon rind in a bowl. Set aside while you make the risotto.

2 Put the saffron strands in a small bowl. Pour over the boiling water and leave to stand. Melt the butter in a heavy-based saucepan and gently fry the onion for 3 minutes, until softened.

3 Stir in the rice and cook, stirring all the time, for about 2 minutes until it becomes translucent. Add the wine and saffron mixture and cook for several minutes until the wine is absorbed.

4 Add 600ml/1 pint/2½ cups of the stock to the pan and simmer gently until the stock is absorbed, stirring frequently.

5 Gradually add more stock, a ladleful at a time, until the rice is tender. (The rice might be tender and creamy before you've added all the stock so add it slowly towards the end of the cooking time.)

6 Season the risotto with salt and pepper and transfer to a serving dish. Scatter lavishly with shavings of Parmesan cheese or grated Parmesan and the gremolata.

> ### COOK'S TIP
> This is a quick and easy version of the famous Risotto alla Milanese, and takes a few liberties with the original. For the sake of speed and simplicity, quite a large quantity of stock is added in the first instance, something that would be sacrilege to any Italian proud of his or her risotto-making skills. In the traditional recipe, the stock would very definitely be home-made and of the finest quality; it would be kept simmering on the stove throughout the cooking process and added lovingly and no more than a ladleful at a time. No new stock would be added until the last ladleful had been absorbed. The risotto would be stirred constantly, and the grains of rice would gradually become plump and creamy. If you have time, it is well worth using the traditional method to make this risotto, but if not, you will still get very good results by making this speedier version.

MUSHROOM AND OKRA CURRY WITH MANGO RELISH

Preparation time 10 minutes
Cooking time 13–18 minutes

SERVES 4

4 garlic cloves, roughly chopped
2.5cm/1in piece of fresh root ginger,
 peeled and roughly chopped
1–2 red chillies, seeded and chopped
175ml/6fl oz/ ¾ cup cold water
15ml/1 tbsp sunflower oil
5ml/1 tsp coriander seeds
5ml/1 tsp cumin seeds
5ml/1 tsp ground cumin
seeds from 2 green cardamom
 pods, ground
pinch of ground turmeric
400g/14oz can chopped tomatoes
450g/1lb/4 cups mushrooms,
 quartered if large
225g/8oz okra, trimmed and sliced
30ml/2 tbsp chopped fresh coriander
basmati rice, to serve
For the mango relish
1 large ripe mango, about 500g/1¼ lb
1 small garlic clove, crushed
1 onion, finely chopped
10ml/2 tsp grated fresh ginger root
1 fresh red chilli, seeded and finely
 chopped
pinch each of salt and sugar

1 For the mango relish, peel the mango and chop the flesh.

2 In a bowl, mash the mango flesh with a fork and mix in the rest of the relish ingredients. Set aside.

3 Put the garlic, ginger, chillies and 45ml/3 tbsp of the water into a blender or food processor and blend until smooth.

4 Heat the sunflower oil in a large pan. Add the whole coriander and cumin seeds and allow them to sizzle for a few seconds. Add the ground cumin, ground cardamom and turmeric and cook for 1 minute more, until aromatic.

5 Add the garlic paste from the blender or food processor, the tomatoes, remaining water, mushrooms and okra. Stir to mix well and bring to the boil. Reduce the heat, cover, and simmer the mixture for 5 minutes.

6 Remove the cover, turn up the heat slightly and cook for another 5–10 minutes until the okra is tender. Stir in the fresh coriander and serve with rice and the mango relish.

LEEK AND CARAWAY GRATIN WITH A CARROT CRUST

Tender leeks are mixed with a creamy caraway sauce and a crunchy carrot topping to make a simply superb supper.

Preparation and
cooking time 28–30 minutes

SERVES 4–6
675g/1½ lb leeks, cut into
  7.5cm/3in pieces
150ml/¼ pint/⅔ cup vegetable stock
  or water
45ml/3 tbsp dry white wine
5ml/1 tsp caraway seeds
pinch of salt
300ml/½ pint/1¼ cups milk,
  as required
25g/1oz/2 tbsp butter
25g/1oz/¼ cup plain flour
For the topping
175g/6oz/2 cups fresh wholemeal
  breadcrumbs
115g/4oz/1 cup grated carrot
30ml/2 tbsp chopped fresh parsley
75g/3oz Jarlsberg cheese,
  coarsely grated
25g/1oz/2 tbsp slivered almonds

1   Place the leeks in a large pan.
Add the stock or water, wine,
caraway seeds and salt. Bring to a
simmer, cover and cook for about
5 minutes until the leeks are
just tender.

2   With a slotted spoon, transfer
the leeks to an ovenproof dish.
Reduce the remaining liquid to half
then make the amount up to 350ml/
12fl oz/1½ cups with milk.

3   Preheat the oven to 190°C/
375°F/Gas 5. Melt the butter
in a saucepan, stir in the flour and
cook without allowing it to colour
for 1 minute. Gradually add the stock
and milk, stirring well after each
addition, until the sauce boils and
thickens. Pour the creamy sauce
over the leeks in the dish and level
the surface.

4   Mix all the topping ingredients
together in a bowl and sprinkle
over the leeks. Bake in the oven for
15 minutes until golden.

TAGLIATELLE WITH SPRING VEGETABLE SAUCE

A creamy pea sauce makes a wonderful combination with the crunchy young vegetables.

Preparation time 4 minutes
Cooking time 22 minutes

SERVES 4

15ml/1 tbsp olive oil
1 garlic clove, crushed
6 spring onions, sliced
225g/8oz/2 cups frozen peas, thawed
350g/12oz fresh young asparagus
30ml/2 tbsp chopped fresh sage, plus
*   extra leaves to garnish*
finely grated rind of 2 lemons
450ml/ ³/₄ pint/scant 2 cups vegetable
*   stock or water*
225g/8oz/2 cups frozen broad
*   beans, thawed*
450g/1lb fresh or dried tagliatelle
60ml/4 tbsp natural yogurt

COOK'S TIP

Frozen peas and beans have been used here to cut down the preparation time, but the dish tastes even better if you use fresh young vegetables when in season.

1 Heat the oil in a pan. Add the garlic and spring onions and cook gently, stirring occasionally, for 2–3 minutes until softened.

2 Add the peas and one-third of the asparagus, with the sage, lemon rind and stock or water. Bring to the boil, reduce the heat and simmer for 10 minutes until tender. Purée in a blender until smooth.

3 Meanwhile remove the outer skins from the broad beans and discard. Set the beans aside.

4 Cut the remaining asparagus in 5cm/2in lengths, trimming off any tough fibrous stems. Blanch in boiling water for 2 minutes.

5 Cook the tagliatelle in a pan of boiling lightly salted water until just tender. Drain well.

6 Scrape the puréed pea mixture into a pan, add the cooked asparagus and shelled beans and reheat. Stir in the yogurt. Tip the tagliatelle into a large bowl, add the sauce and toss well. Garnish with a few extra sage leaves and serve.

LEMON AND GINGER SPICY BEANS

An extremely quick delicious meal, made with canned beans for speed.

Preparation time 6 minutes
Cooking time 17–22 minutes

SERVES 4

5cm/2in piece of fresh root ginger,
   peeled and roughly chopped
3 garlic cloves, roughly chopped
250ml/8fl oz/1 cup cold water
15ml/1 tbsp sunflower oil
1 large onion, thinly sliced
1 red chilli, seeded and chopped
1.5ml/ ¼ tsp cayenne pepper
10ml/2 tsp ground cumin
5ml/1 tsp ground coriander
2.5ml/ ½ tsp ground turmeric
30ml/2 tbsp lemon juice
75g/3oz/1½ cups chopped fresh
   coriander
400g/14oz can black-eyed beans,
   drained and rinsed
400g/14oz can aduki beans, drained
   and rinsed
400g/14oz can haricot beans,
   drained and rinsed
ground black pepper
crusty bread, to serve

1 Place the ginger, garlic and 60ml/4 tbsp of the cold water in a blender; whizz until smooth.

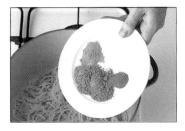

2 Heat the oil in a pan. Add the onion and chilli and cook gently for 5 minutes until softened. Add the cayenne pepper, cumin, coriander and turmeric and stir-fry for 1 minute.

3 Stir in the ginger and garlic paste from the blender and cook for another minute.

4 Add the remaining water, the lemon juice and chopped fresh coriander, stir well and bring to the boil. Cover the pan tightly, lower the heat and cook for 5 minutes.

5 Add all the beans to the pan and cook for 5–10 minutes more. Season with pepper and serve

PIZZA MARINARA

The combination of garlic, good quality olive oil and fresh oregano gives this pizza an unmistakably Italian flavour.

Preparation time 5 minutes
Cooking time 20–25 minutes

SERVES 2–3
60ml/4 tbsp olive oil
675g/1¹/₂lb plum tomatoes, peeled,
  seeded and chopped
1 pizza base, about 25–30cm/
  10–12in diameter
4 garlic cloves, cut into slivers
15ml/1 tbsp chopped fresh oregano
salt and ground black pepper

1 Preheat the oven to 220°C/ 425°F/Gas 7. Heat about 30ml/ 2 tbsp of the oil in a pan. Add the tomatoes and cook for 5 minutes until soft.

2 Transfer the tomatoes to a sieve and leave to drain for about 5 minutes.

3 Place the tomatoes in a food processor or blender and purée until smooth.

4 Brush the pizza base with half the remaining oil. Spoon over the tomatoes and sprinkle with garlic and oregano. Drizzle over the remaining oil and season with salt and a generous grinding of black pepper. Bake for 15–20 minutes until crisp and golden. Serve immediately.

PIZZA MARGHERITA

This classic pizza is simple to prepare. Sun-ripe tomatoes, basil and mozzarella make a good team.

Preparation time 2–3 minutes
Cooking time 15–20 minutes

SERVES 2–3

*1 pizza base, about 25–30cm/
  10–12in diameter
30ml/2 tbsp olive oil
250ml/8fl oz/1 cup ready-made
  tomato sauce
150g/5oz mozzarella cheese
2 ripe tomatoes, thinly sliced
6–8 fresh basil leaves
30ml/2 tbsp freshly grated
  Parmesan cheese
ground black pepper*

1 Preheat the oven to 220ºC/
425ºF/Gas 7. Brush the pizza base with 15ml/1 tbsp of the oil and then spread over the tomato sauce, taking it to the edges.

2 Cut the mozzarella cheese into thin slices.

3 Arrange the sliced mozzarella and tomatoes on top of the pizza base. They look very attractive in concentric circles, with alternate slices of tomato and cheese.

4 Roughly tear the basil leaves, add and sprinkle with the Parmesan. Drizzle over the remaining oil and season with black pepper. Bake for 15–20 minutes until crisp and golden. Serve immediately.

CHERRY PANCAKES

Pancakes provide the perfect answer to the question of what to serve for pudding when there's very little time. The ingredients are all store cupboard basics, even the fruit.

Preparation time 4 minutes
Cooking time 18 minutes

SERVES 4

50g/2oz/ ½ cup plain flour
50g/2oz/ ½ cup plain wholemeal
  flour
pinch of salt
1 egg, beaten
150ml/ ¼ pint/ ⅔ cup milk
150ml/ ¼ pint/ ⅔ cup water
a little oil for frying
For the filling
425g/15oz can black cherries in juice
7.5ml/1½ tsp arrowroot
double cream, crème fraîche or Greek
  yogurt, to serve

1 Sift the flours and salt into a bowl, adding any bran left in the sieve to the bowl at the end.

COOK'S TIPS

If fresh cherries are in season, cook them gently in enough apple juice just to cover them, and then thicken the juice with arrowroot as in Step 5.

The basic pancakes will freeze very successfully. Interleave them with non-stick or absorbent kitchen paper, overwrap them in polythene and seal. Freeze for up to six months. Thaw at room temperature.

2 Make a well in the centre of the flour and add the beaten egg. Gradually beat in the milk and water, whisking hard until all the liquid is incorporated and the batter is smooth and bubbly.

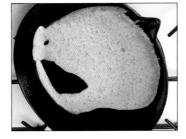

3 Heat a small non-stick frying pan with a small amount of oil until the pan is very hot. Pour in just enough batter to cover the base of the pan, swirling the pan to cover the base evenly.

4 Cook until the pancake is set and golden, and then turn to cook the other side. Slide on to a sheet of kitchen paper; make seven more pancakes.

5 Drain the cherries, reserving the juice. Blend about 30ml/2 tbsp of the juice from the can of cherries with the arrowroot in a saucepan. Stir in the rest of the juice. Heat gently, stirring, until boiling.

6 Stir the mixture over a medium heat for about 2 minutes, until it thickens and clears. Add the cherries and stir until thoroughly heated. Spoon the cherries into the pancakes and fold them in quarters. Serve at once, with double cream, crème fraîche or Greek yogurt, if you like.

NECTARINE PUFF PASTRY TARTS

These delicious, yet simple, fresh fruit pastries are easy to put together, but the puff pastry makes them seem very elegant.

Preparation time 15 minutes
Cooking time 12–15 minutes

SERVES 6
*225g/8oz frozen puff
  pastry, thawed
450g/1lb nectarines
15g/ ¹/₂oz/1 tbsp butter
30ml/2 tbsp caster sugar
freshly grated nutmeg
crème fraîche or lightly whipped
  cream, to serve (optional)*

[1] Lightly butter a large baking sheet and sprinkle very lightly with water.

[2] On a lightly floured surface, roll out the puff pastry to a large rectangle, about 40 × 25cm/16 × 10in and cut into six smaller rectangles.

COOK'S TIP
Use ready-rolled puff pastry for speed.

[3] Transfer to the baking sheet. Using the back of a small knife, scallop the edges of the pastry. Then using the tip of the knife, score a line 1cm/¹/₂in from the edge of each rectangle to form a border. Preheat the oven to 200°C/400°F/Gas 6.

[4] Cut the nectarines in half and remove the stones, then slice the fruit thinly. Arrange the nectarine slices down the centre of the rectangles, leaving the borders on each uncovered. Sprinkle the fruit with the sugar and a little nutmeg.

[5] Bake for 12–15 minutes until the edges of the pastry are puffed and the fruit is tender. Transfer the tarts to a wire rack to cool slightly. Serve warm with a little crème fraîche or lightly whipped cream, if you like.

MEXICAN FRITTERS

Preparation time 15 minutes
Cooking time 12–15 minutes

SERVES 6

225g/8oz/2 cups plain flour
5ml/1 tsp baking powder
2.5ml/ ½ tsp salt
15ml/1 tbsp granulated sugar
1 egg, beaten
120ml/4fl oz/ ½ cup milk
25g/1oz/2 tbsp butter, melted
oil, for frying
sugar for dusting
For the syrup
225g/8oz/1⅓ cups soft light
  brown sugar
750ml/1¼ pints/3 cups water
2.5cm/1in cinnamon stick
1 clove

1   Make the syrup. Combine all the ingredients in a saucepan. Heat, stirring, until the sugar has dissolved, then simmer until the mixture has reduced to a light syrup. Discard the spices. Keep the syrup warm while you make the fritters.

2   Sift the flour, baking powder and salt. Stir in the sugar. Whisk the egg and the milk together. Gradually stir in the dry mixture. Beat in the butter to make a soft dough.

3   Turn the dough on to a lightly floured board and knead until it is smooth and elastic. Divide the dough into 18 even-size pieces. Shape into balls, then flatten to disc shapes about 2cm/¾in thick.

4   Use the floured handle of a wooden spoon to poke a hole through the centre of each fritter. Pour oil into a deep frying pan to a depth of 5cm/2in. Alternatively, use a deep-fryer. Heat the oil to 190°C/375°F or until a small cube of day-old bread added to the oil turns golden brown in 30–60 seconds.

5   Fry the fritters in batches, taking care not to overcrowd the pan, until they are puffy and golden brown on both sides. Lift out with a slotted spoon and drain on kitchen paper.

6   Dust the fritters with sugar and serve with the syrup.

COOK'S TIP
If you remember, make the syrup ahead of time, chilling it until needed, then warming it through quickly at the same time as you fry the fritters.

BLUEBERRY AND ORANGE CRÊPE BASKETS

Impress your guests with these pretty, fruit-filled crêpes. When blueberries are out of season, replace them with other soft fruit, such as raspberries or strawberries.

Preparation time 5 minutes
Cooking time 16–23 minutes

SERVES 6

150g/5oz/1¼ cups plain flour
pinch salt
2 egg whites
200ml/7fl oz/scant 1 cup milk
150ml/¼ pint/⅔ cup orange juice
Greek yogurt, crème fraîche, or
whipped cream, to serve
For the filling
4 medium oranges
225g/8oz/2 cups blueberries

1 Preheat the oven to 200°C/400°F/Gas 6. To make the pancakes, sift the flour and salt into a bowl. Make a well in the centre of the flour and add the egg whites, milk and orange juice. Whisk hard, until all the liquid has been incorporated and the batter is smooth and bubbly. Pour it into a jug.

COOK'S TIPS
You'll need to work quickly to make this dessert in half an hour. If you can, make the batter ahead of time: it will improve on standing. Stir it before cooking the pancakes. Fill the pancake baskets seconds before serving, or they will absorb the fruit juice and start to soften.

2 Lightly grease a heavy or non-stick pancake pan and heat it until it is very hot. Pour in just enough batter to cover the base of the pan, swirling it to cover the base of the pan evenly.

3 Cook for 1–2 minutes until the pancake has set and is brown underneath, then turn it to cook the other side. Slide the pancake on to a sheet of kitchen paper, and then cook the rest of the batter, to make at least six pancakes, in all.

4 Place six small ovenproof bowls or moulds on a baking sheet and drape the pancakes over these. Bake them in the oven for about 10 minutes, until they are crisp and set into shape. Carefully lift the "baskets" off the moulds.

5 Meanwhile, pare a thin piece of orange rind from one orange and cut it in fine strips. Blanch the strips in boiling water for 30 seconds, rinse them in cold water, drain them and set them aside.

6 Cut the peel and pith from all the oranges. Divide the oranges into segments, catching the juice in a pan. Add the orange segments and blueberries to the pan and warm the mixture gently. Spoon the fruit into the baskets and scatter the shreds of rind over the top. Serve immediately with yogurt, crème fraîche or cream.

CORNFLAKE-TOPPED PEACH BAKE

Make this simple family pudding in minutes, using familiar store cupboard ingredients.

Preparation time 2 minutes
Cooking time 20 minutes

SERVES 4

*400g/14oz can peach slices
   in juice
30ml/2 tbsp sultanas
1 cinnamon stick
strip of fresh orange rind
25g/1oz/2 tbsp butter
50g/2oz/1½ cups cornflakes
15ml/1 tbsp sesame seeds*

[1] Preheat the oven to 200°C/ 400°F/Gas 6. Drain the canned peach slices, reserving the juice, and then arrange them in a shallow ovenproof dish.

[2] Place the peach juice, sultanas, cinnamon stick and orange rind in a pan and bring to the boil. Lower the heat and simmer for 3–4 minutes, to reduce the liquid by about half. Remove the cinnamon stick and orange rind and spoon the syrup over the peaches.

[3] Melt the butter in a small pan and stir in the cornflakes and sesame seeds.

[4] Spread the cornflake mixture over the fruit. Bake for about 15 minutes, or until the topping is crisp and golden. Serve hot.

SUMMER BERRY SPONGE TART

*When soft fruits are in season, try
making this delicious sponge tart.
Serve warm from the oven with
scoops of vanilla ice cream.*

Preparation time 10 minutes
Cooking time 15 minutes

SERVES 4–6
softened butter, for greasing
*450g/1lb/4 cups soft fruit, such as
    raspberries, blackberries,
    blackcurrants, redcurrants,
    strawberries or blueberries*
2 eggs, at room temperature
*about 50g/2oz/ ¼ cup caster
    sugar*
15ml/1 tbsp plain flour
*50g/2oz/ ½ cup ground almonds
    or hazelnuts*
vanilla ice cream, to serve

1   Preheat the oven to 190ºC/
375ºF/Gas 5. Brush a 23cm/9in
flan tin with softened butter and line
the bottom with a circle of non-stick
baking paper. Scatter the fruit in the
bottom of the tin, adding a little sugar
if the fruit is tart.

COOK'S TIPS
When time is short (or the soft fruit
season has passed) use bottled fruits,
but make sure they are well drained
before use. To continue the almond
theme, you could decorate the tart just
before serving with a scattering of
toasted almonds.

2   Whisk the eggs and sugar
together for 3–4 minutes or
until the whisk leaves a thick trail
across the surface. Combine the flour
and almonds or hazelnuts, then fold
into the egg mixture with a spatula,
retaining as much air as possible.

3   Spread the mixture on top of
the fruit base. Bake for about
15 minutes or until the sponge has
set. Remove the tart from the tin and
transfer to a serving plate. Serve
warm with vanilla ice cream.

FRUITY RICOTTA CREAMS

Ricotta is an Italian soft cheese with a smooth texture and a mild, slightly sweet flavour. Served here with candied fruit peel and delicious chocolate – it is quite irresistible.

Preparation time 25 minutes
Cooking time Nil

SERVES 4
350g/12oz/1½ cups ricotta
30–45ml/2–3 tbsp Cointreau or other
   orange liqueur
10ml/2 tsp grated lemon rind
30ml/2 tbsp icing sugar
150ml/ ¼ pint/ ⅔ cup double cream
150g/5oz candied peel, such as
   orange, lemon and citron,
   finely chopped
50g/2oz plain chocolate,
   finely chopped
chocolate curls, to decorate
amaretti biscuits, to serve (optional)

1 Using the back of a wooden spoon, push the ricotta through a fine sieve into a large bowl.

2 Add the liqueur, lemon rind and sugar and beat well until the mixture is light and smooth.

3 Whip the cream in a large bowl until it forms soft peaks.

4 Gently fold the cream into the ricotta mixture with the candied peel and chopped chocolate.

5 Spoon the mixture into four glass serving dishes and chill until ready to serve. Decorate with chocolate curls and serve with amaretti biscuits, if you like.

HOT FRUIT WITH MAPLE BUTTER

Preparation time 20 minutes
Cooking time 10 minutes

SERVES 4
1 large papaya, halved
2 bananas
115g/4oz/ ½ cup butter, diced
60ml/4 tbsp pure maple syrup
1 large mango, peeled and sliced
1 small pineapple, peeled and cubed

1 Scoop out the seeds from the papaya, slice and peel.

2 Peel the bananas, then cut them in half lengthways.

3 Put the butter and maple syrup in a food processor and whizz until smooth and creamy, scraping down the sides of the processor bowl once or twice if necessary. Scrape the maple butter into a bowl and set it aside. (A hand-held blender is ideal for the job and you only need one bowl.)

4 Mix the bananas and papaya in a gratin dish, cutting the papaya slices into chunks if you prefer. Add the mango and pineapple and mix gently. Preheat the grill.

5 Grill the fruit under a medium heat for 10 minutes or until tender, turning it occasionally and brushing it frequently with the maple butter.

6 Arrange the fruit on a warmed serving platter and dot with the remaining maple butter. Sprinkle over a little ground cinnamon, if you like and serve the fruit piping hot.

COOK'S TIP
Be sure to use pure maple syrup, as imitations have little of the taste of the real thing.

CRÊPES SUZETTE WITH COINTREAU AND COGNAC

Thin pancakes filled with Cointreau-flavoured butter and flambéed with Cognac may be a classic, but they remain as popular as ever.

Preparation time 8–10 minutes
Cooking time 14 minutes

SERVES 6

115g/4oz/1 cup plain flour
2.5ml/ ½ tsp salt
2 eggs, beaten
300ml/ ½ pint/1¼ cups milk
oil, for frying
juice of 2 oranges
45ml/3 tbsp Cognac
icing sugar, for dusting
strips of thinly pared orange rind,
*   to decorate*

For the orange butter
175g/6oz/ ¾ cup unsalted butter
50g/2oz/ ¼ cup granulated sugar
grated rind of 2 oranges
30ml/2 tbsp Cointreau

[1] Make the orange butter. Cream the butter with the sugar, orange rind and Cointreau. Set aside while you make the pancake batter.

[2] Sift the flour and salt into a bowl, make a well in the centre and beat in the eggs. Gradually stir in the milk and beat to a smooth batter. Pour into a jug. Heat the oil in a pan, pour in a little batter and make a thin pancake. Cook until the underside is golden, turn over and cook the other side. Slide out of the pan. Make at least five more pancakes.

[3] Spread the pancakes with half the orange butter and fold into neat quarters.

[4] Heat the rest of the orange butter in a frying pan with the orange juice, add all the folded pancakes and turn them carefully to heat them through. Push the pancakes to one side of the pan and pour in the Cognac. Heat, then carefully set alight. When the flames die down, spoon the sauce over the pancakes. Serve immediately, dusted with icing sugar and decorated with strips of orange rind.

COOK'S TIP
Not traditional, but equally delicious, is to use rum in place of the Cointreau and Cognac, and add sliced fresh pineapple and a little toasted coconut.

CHOCOLATE SOUFFLÉS

These soufflés are easy to make and can be prepared in advance if you can spare the time — the filled dishes can wait for up to one hour before baking. Use good quality Continental chocolate.

Preparation time 10 minutes
Cooking time 18–20 minutes

SERVES 6
175g/6oz plain chocolate, chopped
150g/5oz/⅔ cup unsalted butter, cut in small pieces
4 large eggs, separated
30ml/2 tbsp orange liqueur (optional)
1.5ml/¼ tsp cream of tartar
45ml/3 tbsp caster sugar
icing sugar, for dusting
For the white chocolate sauce
90ml/6 tbsp whipping cream
75g/3oz white chocolate, chopped
15–30ml/1–2 tbsp orange liqueur
grated rind of ½ orange

1 Generously butter six 150ml/ ¼ pint/⅔ cup ramekins. Sprinkle each with a little caster sugar and tap out any excess. Put the ramekins on a baking sheet.

2 In a heavy saucepan over a very low heat, melt the chocolate and butter, stirring until smooth. Remove from the heat and cool slightly, then beat in the egg yolks and orange liqueur, if using. Set aside, stirring occasionally.

3 Preheat the oven to 220°C/ 425°F/Gas 7. In a clean grease-free bowl, whisk the egg whites slowly until frothy. Add the cream of tartar, increase the speed and whisk until they form soft peaks. Gradually sprinkle over the sugar, 15ml/1 tbsp at a time, whisking until the whites are stiff and glossy.

4 Stir a third of the whites into the cooled chocolate mixture to lighten it, then pour the chocolate mixture over the remaining whites. Using a rubber spatula or large metal spoon, gently fold the sauce into the whites. (Don't worry about a few white streaks.) Spoon into the prepared dishes and put them back on the baking sheet. Bake for 10–12 minutes, until well risen.

5 Meanwhile, make the white chocolate sauce. Put the chocolate and cream into a small saucepan. Stir over a low heat until melted and smooth. Remove from the heat and stir in the liqueur and orange rind, then pour into a serving jug. Serve the soufflés as soon as they are cooked, dusted with icing sugar and accompanied by the sauce.

AMARETTO SOUFFLÉ

Preparation and cooking time 30 minutes

SERVES 6

105ml/7 tbsp caster sugar
6 amaretti biscuits, coarsely crushed
90ml/6 tbsp Amaretto liqueur
4 eggs, separated, plus 1 egg white
30ml/2 tbsp plain flour
250ml/8fl oz/1 cup milk
pinch of cream of tartar (if needed)
icing sugar, for dusting

1 Preheat the oven to 200°C/400°F/Gas 6. Thoroughly butter a 1.5 litre/2½ pint/6¼ cup soufflé dish and sprinkle it with a little of the caster sugar.

2 Put the crushed amaretti biscuits in a bowl. Sprinkle them with 30ml/2 tbsp of the Amaretto liqueur and set aside while you make the soufflé base.

3 Mix the egg yolks, flour and 30ml/2 tbsp of the sugar.

4 Heat the milk in a heavy pan. When it is almost boiling, stir it in to the egg mixture, stirring.

5 Pour the mixture back into the pan. Put over a low heat and simmer gently for 3–4 minutes or until thickened, stirring occasionally. Remove from the heat and gradually add the remaining Amaretto liqueur, stirring all the time.

6 In a grease-free bowl, whisk the 5 egg whites until they will hold soft peaks. (If not using a copper bowl, add the cream of tartar as soon as the whites are frothy.) Add the remaining sugar and continue whisking until stiff.

7 Add about one-quarter of the whites to the liqueur mixture and stir in with a rubber spatula. Add the remaining whites and fold in gently.

8 Spoon half of the mixture into the prepared soufflé dish. Cover with a layer of the moistened amaretti biscuits, then spoon the remaining soufflé mixture on top.

9 Bake for 20 minutes or until the soufflé is risen and lightly browned. Sprinkle with sifted icing sugar and serve immediately.

COOK'S TIP
Some people like soufflés to be completely cooked. Others prefer a soft, creamy centre. The choice is up to you. To check how cooked the middle is, insert a thin skewer into the centre: it will come out almost clean or with some moist particles clinging to it.

CINNAMON AND APRICOT SOUFFLÉS

Don't expect this to be difficult simply because it's a soufflé — it really couldn't be easier.

Preparation time 15 minutes
Cooking time 12–15 minutes

SERVES 4
flour, for dusting
3 eggs
115g/4oz/ ¹/₂ cup apricot fruit spread
finely grated rind of ¹/₂ lemon
5ml/1 tsp ground cinnamon, plus
*   extra to decorate*

1   Preheat the oven to 190°C/
375°F/Gas 5. Lightly grease
four individual soufflé dishes and
dust them lightly with flour.

2   Separate the eggs, placing the
yolks in one bowl and the
whites in a second, grease-free bowl.
Add the apricot fruit spread, grated
lemon rind and cinnamon to the
egg yolks.

3   Using a hand-held electric
mixer, whisk the egg yolk
mixture hard until it is thick and pale
in colour. Whisk the egg whites with
clean beaters until they are stiff
enough to hold soft peaks.

4   Using a metal spoon or spatula,
fold the egg whites evenly into
the yolk mixture. Spoon into the
prepared dishes. Bake the soufflés for
12–15 minutes, until well risen and
lightly browned. Serve at once.

INDEX

A

Amaretto soufflé, 250
apples: apple soufflé omelette, 165
  cabbage slaw with date and, 70
  curried carrot and apple soup, 180
  smoked mackerel and apple dip, 102
apricots: cinnamon and apricot
    soufflés, 251
  quick apricot blender whip, 88
  warm bagels with poached
    apricots, 81
artichokes: French bread pizzas
    with, 147
  pasta with broccoli and, 160
  prosciutto, mushroom and artichoke
    pizza, 204
asparagus: asparagus rolls with herb
    butter sauce, 106
  spinach tagliarini with, 55
  tagliatelle with prosciutto and, 52
  with orange sauce, 105
  with tarragon butter, 24
avgolemono, 14
avocados: avocado and papaya
    salad, 111
  guacamole, 26

B

bacon: bacon koftas, 198
  chicken, bacon and corn kebabs, 192
  curly endive salad with, 62
  spaghetti alla carbonara, 54
  spinach salad with prawns and, 58
bagels, warm, with poached
    apricots, 81
balti mushrooms in a creamy garlic
    sauce, 75
bananas: Brazilian coffee, 82
  with rum and raisin, 83
beans: lemon and ginger spicy
    beans, 235
  mixed bean salad with tomato
    dressing, 72
  pasta and bean soup, 179
beef: beef and mushroom
    burgers, 203
  beef strips with orange and
    ginger, 115
  chilli beef nachos, 100
  pepper steaks with chive butter and
    brandy, 196

  Stilton beefburgers, 113
beetroot: beetroot and herring
    salad, 184
  spinach and beetroot salad, 152
blueberry and orange crêpe
    baskets, 242
Brazilian coffee bananas, 82
brioche with mixed mushrooms, 148
broad bean and feta salad, warm, 64
broccoli: broccoli and cauliflower
    gratin, 150
  haddock and broccoli chowder, 98
  pasta with artichokes and, 160
buckwheat noodles *see* noodles

C

cabbage: slaw with date and apple, 70
  Thai-style cabbage salad, 61
Caesar salad, 59
Cajun-spiced chicken, 123
Cajun-spiced fish, 144
calf's liver with honey, 40
Caribbean chicken kebabs, 122
carrots: carrot and coriander
    soup, 176
  curried carrot and apple soup, 180
  lemon carrot salad, 228
cashew nuts: cashew chicken, 32
  Chinese chicken with, 190
cauliflower: broccoli and cauliflower
    gratin, 150
  creamy cauliflower and walnut
    soup, 180
cheese: broccoli and cauliflower
    gratin, 150
  buckwheat noodles with goat's
    cheese, 76
  cheese-stuffed pears, 187

  ciabatta with mozzarella and grilled
    onion, 29
  eggs with spinach and cheese
    sauce, 225
  French goat's cheese salad, 56
  Greek salad pittas, 56
  halloumi and grape salad, 64
  hot tomato and mozzarella salad, 24
  lemon and Parmesan capellini with
    herb bread, 158
  melting cheese dip, 28
  pizza Margherita, 237
  pork with Camembert, 42
  potato cakes with goat's cheese, 227
  quick pitta pizzas, 146
  ravioli with four-cheese sauce, 53
  salad leaves with Gorgonzola, 30
  Stilton beefburgers, 113
  three-cheese croûtes, 156
  tomato and mozzarella toasts, 30
  Turkish salad, 66
  warm broad bean and feta salad, 64
  see also ricotta
cherry pancakes, 238
chick-peas: hummus, 27
chicken: Cajun-spiced, 123
  Caribbean chicken kebabs, 122
  cashew chicken, 32
  chicken, bacon and corn kebabs, 192
  chicken chow mein, 121
  chicken paella, 194
  Chinese chicken with cashew
    nuts, 190
  in creamy orange sauce, 189
  stir-fried chicken with basil and
    chillies, 33
  tandoori chicken kebabs, 190
  Thai chicken and vegetable
    stir-fry, 34
  Thai chicken soup, 178
  warm chicken and vegetable
    salad, 124
  with tomatoes and olives, 35
  see also liver
chilli prawns, 142
Chinese chicken with cashew
    nuts, 190
Chinese garlic mushrooms, 182
chocolate: chocolate fudge sundaes, 91
  chocolate sauce, 9
  chocolate soufflés, 249

chorizo in olive oil, 20
chowder *see* soup
ciabatta with mozzarella and grilled
    onion, 29
cinnamon and apricot soufflés, 251
citrus green leaf salad, 72
coconut milk, curried prawns in, 206
cod: Cajun-spiced fish, 144
    cod Creole, 128
    crunchy-topped cod, 220
    with caper sauce, 126
corn *see* sweetcorn
corned beef and egg hash, 112
cornflake-topped peach bake, 244
courgette puffs with mixed leaf
    salad, 155
crab: corn and crab chowder, 99
    egg and tomato salad with, 108
cracked wheat and fennel salad, 151
crêpes *see* pancakes
cucumber raita, skewered lamb
    with, 200
curly endive salad with bacon, 62
curries: curried carrot and apple
    soup, 180
    curried prawns in coconut milk, 206
    green prawn curry, 47
    Kashmiri coconut fish curry, 214
    mushroom and okra curry with
    mango relish, 232
    pineapple curry with prawns and
    mussels, 206

D
dates, cabbage slaw with apple
    and, 70
dips, 26–8, 102, 192
duck breasts with Calvados, 195

E
eggs: avgolemono, 14
    baked eggs with creamy leeks, 186
    baked eggs with tarragon, 103
    corned beef and egg hash, 112
    egg and tomato salad with crab, 108
    mixed pepper pipérade, 149
    poached eggs with spinach, 104
    spaghetti alla carbonara, 54
    with spinach and cheese
    sauce, 225
see also frittata; omelettes

emerald fruit salad, 80
Eton mess, 84

F
fennel: cracked wheat and fennel
    salad, 151
    grilled sea bass with, 213
    figs with ricotta cream, 79
fish: fish balls in tomato sauce, 130
    five-spice fish, 128
    seafood pilaff, 132
    spicy fish rösti, 210
    see also cod; tuna etc
five-spice fish, 128
French beans, kedgeree with
    mushrooms and, 163
French bread pizzas with
    artichokes, 147
French goat's cheese salad, 56
frittata: potato and red pepper, 226
    salmon, courgette and
    sweetcorn, 222
fruit: fruity ricotta creams, 246
    hot fruit with maple butter, 246
    red fruit filo baskets, 164
    summer berry sponge tart, 245
fruit salads: cool green, 168
    emerald, 80
    melon and strawberry, 78

G
garlic: balti mushrooms in a creamy
    garlic sauce, 75
    Chinese garlic mushrooms, 182
    garlic baked tomatoes, 228
    garlic prawns, 20
    garlic prawns in filo tartlets, 184
    Spanish garlic soup, 96

gazpacho sauce, turkey rolls
    with, 188
grapefruit: melon and grapefruit
    cocktail, 18
Greek salad pittas, 56
green bean and sweet red pepper
    salad, 63
guacamole, 26

H
haddock: crumbly fish and prawn
    bake, 220
    Kashmiri coconut fish curry, 214
    see also smoked haddock
hake, Spanish-style, 136
halibut with tomato vinaigrette, 44
halloumi and grape salad, 64
ham with Madeira sauce, 196
herb omelette with tomato salad, 156
herring and beetroot salad, 184
hummus, 27

I
ice cream: chocolate fudge
    sundaes, 91
    ice cream strawberry shortcake, 85
Italian ricotta pudding, 90

K
Kashmiri coconut fish curry, 214
kebabs: Caribbean chicken, 122
    chicken, bacon and corn, 192
    mackerel with parsley dressing, 131
    monkfish and potato, 216
    pork and pineapple satay, 201
    tandoori chicken, 190
kedgeree with French beans and
    mushrooms, 163
kidneys: veal kidneys with
    mustard, 114

L
lamb: lamb chops with mint
    vinaigrette, 118
    pan-fried Mediterranean lamb, 198
    skewered lamb with cucumber
    raita, 200
leeks: baked eggs with creamy
    leeks, 186
    leek and caraway gratin with a carrot
    crust, 233

lemon: avgolemono, 14
   lemon and Parmesan capellini with
      herb bread, 158
lemon grass prawns on crisp noodle
   cake, 218
liver: calf's liver with honey, 40
   lamb's liver with peppers, 116
   pan-fried chicken liver salad, 16
   warm chicken liver salad, 60

M

mackerel: kebabs with parsley
      dressing, 131
   with mustard and lemon, 140
   see also smoked mackerel
Madeira sauce, ham with, 196
mandarins in orange flower
   syrup, 86
mangoes: mushroom and okra curry
   with mango relish, 232
   Parma ham with mango, 18
maple butter, hot fruit with, 246
mayonnaise, lime, 210
melon: melon and grapefruit
      cocktail, 18
   melon and strawberry salad, 78
   melon, pineapple and grape
      cocktail, 22
menus, 10–11
Mexican fritters, 241
monkfish and potato kebabs, 216
mushrooms: balti mushrooms in a
      creamy garlic sauce, 75
   beef and mushroom burgers, 203
   brioche with mixed
      mushrooms, 148
   Chinese garlic mushrooms, 182
   kedgeree with French beans
      and, 163
   mushroom and herb soup, 175
   mushroom and okra curry, 232
   prosciutto, mushroom and artichoke
      pizza, 204
mussels: pan-steamed mussels with
      Thai herbs, 141
   pineapple curry with prawns
      and, 206
   tagliatelle with saffron
      mussels, 127
   with cream and parsley, 183
   with wine and garlic, 214

N

nachos, chilli beef, 100
nectarines: grilled with ricotta and
      spice, 171
   puff pastry tarts, 240
noodles: buckwheat noodles with
      goat's cheese, 76
   buckwheat noodles with smoked
      salmon, 50
   chicken chow mein, 121
   lemon grass prawns on crisp noodle
      cake, 218
   prawn noodle salad with fragrant
      herbs, 68
   Thai noodle salad, 69
   vegetable and egg noodle ribbons, 76
   with pineapple, ginger and
      chillies, 50

O

okra and mushroom curry, 232
omelettes: apple soufflé, 165
   herb with tomato salad, 156
orange: blueberry and orange crêpe
      baskets, 242
   chicken in creamy orange
      sauce, 189
   crêpes Suzette with Cointreau and
      Cognac, 248
   orange yogurt brûlées, 170
   prune and orange pots, 169
   watercress and orange soup, 174

P

paella, chicken, 194
pancakes, 9
   blueberry and orange crêpe
      baskets, 242

cherry pancakes, 238
   crêpes Suzette with Cointreau and
      Cognac, 248
papaya: avocado and papaya salad, 111
   papaya skewers with passion fruit
      coulis, 87
Parma ham with mango, 18
passion fruit: papaya skewers with
      passion fruit coulis, 87
   raspberry and passion fruit
      swirls, 89
pasta, 8
   lemon and Parmesan capellini with
      herb bread, 158
   pasta and bean soup, 179
   salmon pasta with parsley
      sauce, 132
   with broccoli and artichokes, 160
   with scallops in tomato sauce, 209
   with spring vegetables, 161
   see also spaghetti; tagliatelle etc
pea soup, fresh, 97
peach bake, cornflake-topped, 244
peanut butter: pork and pineapple
      satay, 201
   vegetable and satay salad, 154
pears: cheese-stuffed pears, 187
   warm pears in cider, 166
pepper steaks with chive butter and
      brandy, 196
peppercorns: salmon with green
      peppercorns, 43
peppers: green bean and sweet red
      pepper salad, 63
   lamb's liver with, 116
   mixed pepper pipérade, 149
   potato and red pepper frittata, 226
   red pepper soup with chilli and
      lime, 95
   turkey rolls with gazpacho sauce, 188
   turkey with yellow pepper sauce, 125
Persian salad, 66
pilaff: seafood, 132
   smoked trout, 219
pineapple: melon, pineapple and
      grape cocktail, 22
   noodles with ginger, chillies
      and, 50
   pineapple curry with prawns and
      mussels, 206
   pineapple flambé, 166

pork and pineapple satay, 201
pipérade, mixed pepper, 149
pitta breads: Greek salad pittas, 56
  quick pitta pizzas, 146
pizzas: French bread pizzas with
    artichokes, 147
  mixed seafood pizza, 205
  pizza Margherita, 237
  pizza marinara, 236
  prosciutto, mushroom and artichoke
    pizza, 204
  quick pitta pizzas, 146
  quick scone pizza, 8
pork: fried rice with pork, 202
  pork and pineapple satay, 201
  sweet-and-sour pork, Thai-style, 120
  in sweet-and-sour sauce, 41
  with Camembert, 42
  with marsala and juniper, 119
potatoes: monkfish and potato
    kebabs, 216
  potato and red pepper frittata, 226
  potato cakes with goat's cheese, 227
  spicy fish rösti, 210
prawns: chilli prawns, 142
  crumbly fish and prawn bake, 220
  curried prawns in coconut
    milk, 206
  garlic prawns, 20
  garlic prawns in filo tartlets, 184
  garlicky scallops and prawns, 48
  green prawn curry, 47
  lemon grass prawns on crisp noodle
    cake, 218
  pan-fried prawns in their shells, 138
  pineapple curry with mussels
    and, 206
  prawn and sweetcorn chowder, 176
  prawn and vegetable balti, 46
  prawn noodle salad with fragrant
    herbs, 68
  spinach salad with bacon and, 58
  Thai prawn salad, 144
prosciutto: prosciutto, mushroom and
    artichoke pizza, 204
  tagliatelle with asparagus and, 52
prune and orange pots, 169

R

raita, cucumber, 200
raspberries: Italian ricotta pudding, 90

raspberry and passion fruit
    swirls, 89
raspberry purée, 9
ravioli with four-cheese sauce, 53
red fruit filo baskets, 164
red mullet grilled with rosemary, 138
rice: chicken paella, 194
  fried rice with pork, 202
  kedgeree with French beans and
    mushrooms, 163
  red fried rice, 162
  risotto alla milanese, 230
  seafood pilaff, 132
  smoked trout pilaff, 219
ricotta: figs with ricotta cream, 79
  fruity ricotta creams, 246
  grilled nectarines with spice and, 171
  Italian ricotta pudding, 90
risotto alla milanese, 230
rösti, spicy fish, 210
runner beans with tomatoes, 152

S

salads: avocado and papaya, 111
  beetroot and herring, 184
  Caesar, 59
  citrus green leaf salad, 72
  courgette puffs with mixed leaf
    salad, 155
  cracked wheat and fennel, 151
  curly endive with bacon, 62
  egg and tomato with crab, 108
  French goat's cheese, 56
  Greek salad pittas, 56
  green bean and sweet red
    pepper, 63
  halloumi and grape, 64
  herb omelette with tomato, 156

  hot tomato and mozzarella, 24
  lemon carrot, 228
  mixed bean salad with tomato
    dressing, 72
  pan-fried chicken liver, 16
  Persian, 66
  prawn noodle salad with fragrant
    herbs, 68
  salad leaves with Gorgonzola, 30
  salade Niçoise, 110
  seafood salad Provençale, 216
  smoked trout, 23
  spinach and beetroot, 152
  spinach with bacon and prawns, 58
  sprouted seed, 70
  summer tuna, 108
  Thai noodle, 69
  Thai prawn, 144
  Thai-style cabbage, 61
  Turkish, 66
  vegetable and satay, 154
  warm broad bean and feta, 64
  warm chicken and vegetable, 124
  warm chicken liver, 60
  warm salmon, 134
salmon: salmon, courgette and
    sweetcorn frittata, 222
  salmon pasta with parsley sauce, 132
  spicy fish rösti, 210
  warm salmon salad, 134
  with green peppercorns, 43
  with watercress sauce, 135
  see also smoked salmon
sauces: chocolate, 9
  tomato, 8
scallops: garlicky prawns and, 48
  pasta with scallops in tomato
    sauce, 209
  sautéed scallops, 48
  with ginger, 142
scone pizza, quick, 8
sea bass grilled with fennel, 213
seafood: mixed seafood pizza, 205
  seafood pilaff, 132
  seafood salad Provençale, 216
  spaghetti with seafood sauce, 137
smoked haddock: haddock and
    broccoli chowder, 98
smoked mackerel and apple dip, 102
smoked salmon, buckwheat noodles
    with, 50

smoked trout: pilaff, 219
  salad, 23
sole: breaded sole batons, 101
  goujons with lime mayonnaise, 210
  pan-fried with lemon butter sauce, 45
soufflés: Amaretto, 250
  chocolate, 249
  cinnamon and apricot, 251
soups: avgolemono, 14
  carrot and coriander, 176
  corn and crab chowder, 99
  creamy cauliflower and
    walnut, 180
  curried carrot and apple, 180
  haddock and broccoli chowder, 98
  mushroom and herb, 175
  pasta and bean, 179
  pea, fresh, 97
  prawn and sweetcorn
    chowder, 176
  red pepper with chilli and
    lime, 95
  Spanish garlic, 96
  Thai chicken, 178
  Thai-style corn, 15
  tomato, fresh, with cheese croûtes, 94
  watercress and orange, 174
soured cream dip, turkey sticks
  with, 192
spaghetti: alla carbonara, 54
  with seafood sauce, 137
Spanish garlic soup, 96
Spanish-style hake, 136
spinach: eggs with cheese sauce
  and, 225
  poached eggs with, 104
  salad with bacon and
    prawns, 58
  spinach and beetroot salad, 152
  with raisins and pine nuts, 74
spinach tagliarini with
  asparagus, 55
sprouted seed salad, 70
Stilton beefburgers, 113
strawberries: Eton mess, 84
  ice cream strawberry shortcake, 85
  melon and strawberry salad, 78
  sundaes, chocolate fudge, 91
sweet-and-sour pork,
  Thai-style, 120
sweet-and-sour sauce, pork
  in, 41

sweetcorn: chicken, bacon and corn
  kebabs, 192
  corn and crab chowder, 99
  prawn and sweetcorn chowder, 176
  Thai-style corn soup, 15

T
tagliarini: spinach tagliarini with
  asparagus, 55
tagliatelle: with prosciutto and
  asparagus, 52
  with saffron mussels, 127
  with spring vegetable
    sauce, 234
  with tomatoes and black
    olives, 159
tandoori chicken kebabs, 190
tarts: garlic prawns in filo tartlets, 184
  nectarine puff pastry
    tarts, 240
  summer berry sponge tart, 245
techniques, 8–9
Thai chicken and vegetable
  stir-fry, 34
Thai chicken soup, 178
Thai noodle salad, 69
Thai prawn salad, 144
Thai-style cabbage salad, 61
Thai-style corn soup, 15
tomatoes: chicken with olives
  and, 35
  fish balls in tomato sauce, 130
  fresh tomato soup with cheese
    croûtes, 94
  garlic baked tomatoes, 228
  halibut with tomato vinaigrette, 44
  herb omelette with tomato
    salad, 156

  hot tomato and mozzarella
    salad, 24
  pasta with scallops in tomato
    sauce, 209
  pizza marinara, 236
  runner beans with, 152
  tagliatelle with black olives
    and, 159
  tomato and mozzarella toasts, 30
  tomato sauce, 8
  tuna steaks with pan-fried plum
    tomatoes, 212
trout: pan-fried with
  hazelnuts, 208
  see also smoked trout
tuna: salade Niçoise, 110
  steaks with pan-fried plum
    tomatoes, 212
  summer tuna salad, 108
turkey: escalopes with capers, 36
  turkey rolls with gazpacho
    sauce, 188
  turkey sticks with soured cream
    dip, 192
  with yellow pepper sauce, 125
Turkish salad, 66

V
veal: escalopes with lemon, 37
  escalopes with tarragon, 38
  pan-fried veal chops, 38
  ragout of veal, 116
vegetables: mixed vegetables with
  aromatic seeds, 224
  pasta with spring vegetables, 161
  prawn and vegetable balti, 46
  tagliatelle with spring vegetable
    sauce, 234
  vegetable and egg noodle
    ribbons, 76
  vegetable and satay salad, 154

W
watercress: salmon with watercress
  sauce, 135
  watercress and orange soup, 174
whitebait, deep-fried, 17

Y
yogurt: cucumber raita, 200
  orange yogurt brûlées, 170
  quick apricot blender whip, 88

NOTES

NOTES

NOTES

NOTES

NOTES

NOTES

NOTES

NOTES